IN HINDSIGHT

THE STORY OF HOW TWO SISTERS
HURT, HINDERED, AND HEALED EACH OTHER

IN HINDSIGHT

SHARON BONANNO & LISA SCOTT

Published by Advantage, Charleston, South Carolina.
Member of Advantage Media Group.

ADVANTAGE is a registered trademark, and the Advantage colophon is a trademark of Advantage Media Group, Inc.

Printed in the United States of America.

10 9 8 7 6 5 4 3 2 1

ISBN: 978-1-64225-131-9
LCCN: 2020918937

Cover design by Carly Blake.
Layout design by Mary Hamilton.

To our mother, "Mom," Marion Kosman.

And to anyone who feels alone.

You. Are. Not.

CONTENTS

INTRODUCTION 1

PART ONE 3
An End and a Beginning

CHAPTER ONE 5
Emergency

CHAPTER TWO 15
A Cry for Help

CHAPTER THREE 23
Runaway

CHAPTER FOUR 33
Fathers and Families

CHAPTER FIVE 43
Quitter

CHAPTER SIX 53
Liar, Liar

CHAPTER SEVEN 65
Merry Christmas

CHAPTER EIGHT 75
Deviant Behavior

CHAPTER NINE 83
Paterson

CHAPTER TEN. 93
Colorado

CHAPTER ELEVEN .101
A New Life

CHAPTER TWELVE .115
Wake Up

PART TWO 125
Better Together

CHAPTER THIRTEEN. 127
Recovery

CHAPTER FOURTEEN 143
A Room for Fish

CHAPTER FIFTEEN. 151
Stepmother

CONCLUSION 163

INTRODUCTION

We were sisters once distanced by addiction, although we remained in close geographic proximity. We spent years turning away from each other in different ways, but neither of us ever walked away. One day we turned and saw each other again.

While the stories in this book are true, we acknowledge that they are told from our perspectives. This is the way that we remember the events of our lives. We mean here to tell our own story; and so, while we want to speak honestly about the people who entered and exited our lives, their names and some of their details have been changed to afford them personal protection. They have their own stories to tell. This is our story.

PART ONE

An End and a Beginning

I've learned that people will forget what you said, people will forget what you did, but people will never forget how you made them feel.
—Maya Angelou

CHAPTER ONE
Emergency

Sharon

You may have to fight a battle more than once to win it.
—Margaret Thatcher

Days before the crisis with my sister Lisa became undeniable, I was sitting in my new family room with my husband, Anthony, and our three young children watching Sunday football. Our oldest son, Joe, was four then and happily playing with a favorite model plane on the floor in front of the TV while our two-year-old, Daniella, was in her usual position on the couch next to her dad, legs walked up the back of the sofa, head dangling upside down over the front edge. She's always liked to be in the thick of things, but to be there in her own way. Our youngest, James, and I were on the floor. Everyone except me was dutifully decked out in Jets jerseys. I'm a less enthusiastic fan than the rest of my family, but I love when we are all together, and that new room had space for all of us.

James was just learning to walk then. With the Jets racing the field in the background, James would push himself up into something that resembled a yoga pose, teeter, inch a foot forward, sway as though the solid floor had turned to a gentle sea, then fall gleefully onto the padding of his diaper. It was a balance not only of body and gravity, but of caution and daring—as much a test of his confidence as an assessment of his coordination.

I had spent nearly every morning and afternoon in the family room with my kids since it had been completed. Its construction had taken six months; this was on top of six months of planning, getting a loan, and hiring an architect and contractor. The new family room was a twelve-by-twelve-foot room that bridged the dining room and kitchen. Building it had required an extension of the foundation, weeks of morning-to-evening clamoring of power tools, and a gaping hole in the kitchen that we covered with a thick sheet of plastic. Growth was painful. Two weeks into the construction, scrambling eggs for everyone's breakfast and shouting over the choking plastic tarp to see what kid wanted what kind of cereal, I thought that we should just nail boards over the hole in the kitchen, plant a garden in the partially completed foundation, give up on improvement, and call it done. Instead we moved in with my in-laws, who lived in a nearby town, and stayed for the duration of the building process. We were lucky to have an escape, but the construction still turned our lives upside down for the sake of improvement. It had seemed contradictory. But now, sitting in the completed room with the entire family—Joe launching the plane in his outstretched arm, Daniella cheering along with her dad, James cruising around the room—I felt a sense of contentment.

It was perhaps because we had just completed the family room, and also because things with Lisa were coming to a head, that I had been thinking about the two houses Lisa and I had grown up in: Mom's house, which was organized for us, and Dad's house, where there was not a single picture of Lisa or me on any wall, and where Lisa and I did not have bedrooms but instead slept on a pullout sofa in a communal room that was transformed by day to leave no trace of our occupancy. So much was communicated by those places.

As adults, Lisa and I were in places as different as those two homes. Anthony and I had been married for seven years—we'd met in high school. I was a teacher and a mother. Our days were organized around getting everyone fed, cleaned, and off to wherever they needed to go. Weeks were shaped by swimming lessons, gymnastics, Anthony's football coaching schedule for the town recreation program, morning jogs and coffee with friends, and playdates that popped up on lazy afternoons. The year was structured by the school term and accented by holidays. My life had a routine that made sense to me. I had moved on from the families that I had shared with Lisa to my own tight crew, with our purposeful rituals. I suppose I had let go of my childhood to embrace the childhoods of my children and the adult life that I desired.

Lisa had boyfriends. She had jobs. She had friends. But her labels were less defined than mine. She had not become something that I could name, other than things that were related to me: sister, aunt. That was okay, I told myself. We had always been different.

When my phone rang, Anthony and the kids barely registered the sharp chime over the excitement of the game. But for me, the sound shattered the peace of the family room that had been solidly focused on smoothly landing planes, cheering on the Jets, and the act of holding oneself steady on two feet.

On the other end of the line, Lisa told me that she was in the emergency room in the nearby town of Suffern.

A familiar tightness took hold in my chest. I assumed that her blood sugar was low—her diabetes had been an issue since we were children.

Lisa hung up before I could ask many questions. She said something was wrong with her nose. "I can't breathe," she said.

I was alarmed but not panicked. Lisa's trouble was so consistent by this point that it had become background noise, pushed to the periphery of my vision. This incident, however, was suspicious. Usually when Lisa was sick, she called Mom. Calls to me came when she was in trouble.

For years I had abided Lisa's mishaps and bad luck even as they became more constant and the circumstances more suspect. You wonder how someone can let things get so extreme. From outside the situation, so much is clear. But from within the problem, each day was only slightly worse than the previous. I acclimated. I accepted. I excused.

You wonder how someone can let things get so extreme. From outside the situation, so much is clear. But from within the problem, each day was only slightly worse than the previous.

And now another emergency had landed Lisa in the actual emergency room. I left my children and husband in the calm of the new family room, put on my jacket, and set out in the New Jersey winter for Suffern.

Suffern is a small town less than twenty miles from Glen Rock, the town where Lisa and I grew up, and five miles from Ramsey, where I lived with my family. Although you can see the Manhattan skyline from parts of town, almost nothing in Suffern is over two stories tall. In January it was gray, as though the sky had been erased, leaving only a dirty smudge of graphite.

The hospital in Suffern is suitably sized, a few stories tall and containing only what is absolutely necessary. Through the glass front doors at the entrance, I scanned the waiting area, where people sat in hard plastic chairs under harsh florescent lights slumped and dazed. I didn't see Lisa. I was at first relieved that she was not among the broken, then terrified at the thought that her state was so bad that she'd been a more pressing case than the others. A chill came over me as I entered the emergency room.

Inside I spoke to a nurse, who let me look over the check-in sheet. Lisa hadn't signed in. Anxiety was taking hold. I was thinking that maybe Lisa had meant not that she was already at the emergency room but that she was headed there and hadn't made it. Something was very wrong. I had to find her.

I left the hospital, went to my car, and called her.

She seemed surprised to hear my voice, happy, as though it were a welcome, casual Sunday afternoon chat with her sister. She might have said something as common as "Hello" or "What are you up to?"

"Are you okay?" I asked.

"Yeah," she said. She was fine. I realized then that I had wanted her to be in the emergency room; I wanted her to have been admitted with a real emergency. It was preferable to it all being a lie. It was a terrible feeling: wishing that she were injured rather than telling me she was fine.

The calmness of her tone enraged me. She had not been in the emergency room. It was an ordinary morning. She was not apologetic for pulling me away from my life and into her own. She said she'd had an issue with a guy whom she was working with. She rambled. She didn't mention the emergency room, her diabetes, or an inability to breathe.

Part of me was still hoping that there was an emergency. I wanted a reason to excuse her behavior. But finally, after years of incidents like this, there wasn't one.

I couldn't control my anger. In hindsight I was probably as angry with myself for letting things go as far as they had with Lisa. "Where the hell are you?" I asked.

"I'm here," she said, as though I could see her through the phone, a remark that seemed both evasive and naive. She told me that she was at the hospital. Or somewhere close. "I'm driving," she said.

It was a game of Marco Polo. I roamed the small parking lot and left out the entrance, scanning the lazy surrounding streets for Lisa's Mercury Mountaineer. Then, there she was, just driving. I followed without telling her I was there.

"How the hell could you do this?" I was screaming into the phone, keeping my eye on her vehicle, which drifted occasionally. I was looking out for other cars or people that might be in her path. "What the hell are you doing? Do you have any idea what you've done? How could you be so inconsiderate? What the hell is the matter with you?"

In the brief spaces that I gave her to answer, she lied, telling me that she was headed to a friend's house who lived in the opposite direction. I didn't say that I was tailing her and knew she was lying.

"Where the hell are you going?" I asked again. I was hoping for a different answer, something that I could believe.

She went on again with the same story about the friend. "I'm going to Angelo's house," she said.

Then there was silence. Not because there was nothing to say but because there was so much to say that the words clogged my throat.

I kept following her. I kept the kind of distance that you keep on those streets in small towns—a couple car lengths back—but I wasn't trying to stay out of sight. I kept thinking that she might catch a glimpse of me in her rearview mirror and pull over. But she kept moving. She didn't seem to be going anywhere. We were on a slow-motion chase through the town of Suffern, I the detective following a suspect or the protective detail keeping watch on someone vulnerable. It felt like we were playing a game, taking on the roles of other people, something we would have once done as children.

My thoughts returned to my new family room. On the night that construction was officially finished, my husband and I had stood together in the doorway not saying anything. His arm was around me. I was amazed that the room was complete, that it was so perfect, and that we could return home. But I have always been able to put my mind to something and accomplish it. I'm not easily overwhelmed. I'm a teacher and a planner. I take things step by step and work my way to a goal. I handle things.

We could have called that new room a den, a living room, or a backroom. It's a strange term, "family room," which seems to suggest that somehow every other room in the house is not about family or a representation of how the family functions. The words seem foreign to me when I consider them carefully: family, room. Making room. Giving room. I had spent my adult life creating room for family. It had to do with belonging and settling a life. And then there was Lisa, driving in circles.

She pulled into the drive-through lane of a Burger King. I watched her speak into the machine, pull up to the window, and trade a few dollar bills for a soda. She meandered into some other places. Her route was indirect. She never seemed to be in a hurry. She certainly didn't seem to be having trouble breathing, but I couldn't leave her. Worrying about Lisa was ingrained in my being. I was concerned that her blood sugar was low. I knew that she was probably high. I was aware of the size of her Mountaineer and the erratic way it slowed and sped up, threatening to do damage that could not be repaired. I had to stay with her until I was sure that she was okay, and so I continued to watch her aimless scavenger hunt through Suffern from a distance. It was surreal, almost as though I was watching someone whom I didn't know or catching the middle of movie whose plot or characters I didn't understand.

"Where are you going?" I asked into the phone again, although it was becoming obvious that she wasn't really going anywhere and that she wasn't going to give me a real answer. I didn't know what she was doing, but now I was certain that there wasn't an emergency.

Lisa had been having large and small emergencies for as long as I could remember. I must have known that there would be a breaking point, but in the moment I maintained the status quo. I excused the things she did and found reasons for the inconsistencies in her stories. I could deal with the little bumps in the road that she seemed so often to hit, so long as she kept her larger issues out of sight.

And her larger issues were all but invisible to me, and nothing that I could get a handle on. They were nameless and nonspecific. She had lied about things of small and large consequence since we were children. She had let her diabetes get out of control. She had difficulty keeping a job. She had friends who partied too hard. Beyond that she seemed like she was drifting, agitated, unhappy, and uneasy. She was never truly present in some way. But she also came over for dinner, talked about work, played with her nephews and niece, and laughed with me about the insane construction of our family room.

There was a definition and specificity to her phone call that day that gave substance to the lie and made it irrefutable. The irrational hour that I'd spent tailing her around town and talking to her on the phone could be mapped in a winding line of absurdity and the minutes being counted on my phone. Still, I didn't tell her that I was following her. I didn't demand that she stop her senseless journey. I kept my distance; I followed her until she finally drove home. And when I knew that she would find her way safely inside, I drove back through the ugly winter to the family room where Anthony was still conducting the cheering squad he'd made of our children.

CHAPTER TWO
A Cry for Help

Lisa

You've got to make a conscious choice every day to shed the old—whatever "the old" means for you.
—Sarah Ban Breathnach

It was like being chased by something in the dark. I couldn't see it, but I knew to be terrified. I was running so fast that I couldn't get enough air. When the oxygen came, it pierced my lungs and clenched my chest, making it painful to take another breath. At first all that I could think about was moving. Fast. Keeping ahead of whatever it was that was chasing me. I wasn't thinking about getting away. I wasn't thinking ahead at all. I was just running and trying to breathe.

Eventually my fear evolved into anxiety. I realized that there was no end in sight. Whatever was after me was not letting up, and I couldn't maintain the pace. Every cell in my body was on the verge of collapse. I had to stop. I was afraid to stop. I wanted my limbs to give out. I wanted to collapse. All that I knew how to do was to keep running.

I remember that I didn't sleep that night. Or at least it felt like I didn't sleep. I fell onto my bed and closed my eyes in the winter-dark early morning, and as soon as I had found quiet, the lights screamed on. When I opened my eyes, Mom and Sharon were standing there in my bedroom.

I was living with a friend named Tiffany then. We had bartended together in the past. The bedroom I stayed in was painted the pale pink that toy manufacturers like to give to the inside of a stuffed bunny's ear. The carpet was a speckled blue with gray and white, that flat kind of carpet that is almost institutional or designed for the outdoors—with a short, retracted weave braced against impact rather than meant to absorb. Tiffany was redoing the inside of the house room by room, patching walls and repainting. It was surface repair that disregarded, or even disguised, the ancient wiring and rusting pipe in the walls. In the process of redoing and touching up, the structure no longer felt like a house but just spaces divided by walls. Most of the furniture had been removed, including the lights. It was always dark. My room was sparse anyway.

It seemed like I might be dreaming as I blinked into the brightness—Mom pressed to a wall and Sharon leaning on the dresser directly across from my bed. I couldn't process my bedroom ignited by the overheads, or the hour of the day, or the haziness of my own head. I couldn't think. I could tell that they were angry. I stayed under the covers, as though the quilt could protect me from whatever they were about to launch my way. Then they started talking.

It was strange because it was usually Sharon who did the talking, but now she stood stiff and silent, watching me as though trying to decide who or what I was. It was Mom who was yelling. She was saying "What are you doing?" and "How could you do this to me? How could you do this to Sharon?" and "Are you on drugs?" and again "How could you? How could you? How could you?"

I wasn't fully awake when I screamed back at her. It was a reflex, like a hand jumping away from a hot surface. I sat up and yelled various versions of "Go away" and "Leave me alone" that ended in the repetition of "Shut the fuck up!"

That morning the accosting felt like it had come out of nowhere. It seemed a random attack. In hindsight I can see the events that brought us all to that moment. I still don't remember stealing money from my sister a week earlier, although I believe that I did it—cocaine is expensive. I took less than twenty dollars from her wallet while I was visiting and ran out the door while she was checking her laundry. It wasn't lot of money, but it was enough to be noticed—mostly because she was noticing other things.

Then, a few days later, I'd called Sharon from the parking lot of the emergency room in Suffern. Cocaine was causing horrible problems with my nose. It burned, it bled, and the blood clotted so that I couldn't breathe. I would take scalding showers just to let some air in. I had sat staring through the glass doors into the emergency room, barely able to breathe, and thought about the doctor examining me. As soon as I let them look at me, they would know that I was on drugs. I stayed in the car, mouth open and puffing steam into the cold winter air before eventually driving away.

Finally, just the night previous to Sharon and Mom appearing in my room, I'd called Mom at two-thirty in the morning. She hadn't answered. I'd left a message on her answering machine. I had been crying so fiercely that I could barely put words together. I'd told her nobody was there for me, nobody understood me, nobody cared about me. I'd told her that I was alone. I'd told her that I knew she loved me. I'd said that I wanted to die.

The truth that I understood later was that I was in a deep depression. I felt sad and alone. So alone. Day after day I had breakdowns. They were constant. I would cry. I would write letters to my sister and Mom. I would pray to God when I went to sleep—"Maybe I don't have to wake up"—and I didn't even know if I believed in God. I was too much of a wimp to take my own life. I would look in the Yellow Pages for places where I could get help. I did this every day—the crying, the praying, the searching. Other than finding and doing cocaine, it became my life. It's hard to explain how truly terrible it was, how empty and worthless I believed I was. I was unbelievably sad. I went through the motions of life, but I wasn't there. I was a shell, and the real me shrunk away inside, getting smaller and farther away from the surface so that I was barely there. For a while the drugs made things better, then they only distracted me. Eventually they did nothing but clog my nose. I couldn't go on.

The feeling wasn't new. I felt this way my whole life. All through my twenties, I had thought that there was something wrong with me, but I didn't think it was the drugs. I knew that I felt bad about myself; I felt like nobody understood me, and I didn't fit in anywhere. I always felt so alone. Cocaine stopped my head from telling me that I was crazy and bad. It was pretty good medicine until it stopped working.

When Mom woke and heard me crying on her answering machine, she called Sharon. I suppose that they had been putting the pieces together for a while.

Mom has always come to my defense, especially because I suffered as a child—and still deal today—with juvenile diabetes. Anytime I screwed up in school, or seemed to be acting strangely, or did something rude or inconsiderate, she would say, "She probably meant this … " or "I'm sure that happened because … " or "Her blood sugar is probably low." She never wanted to believe anything bad about me. Even while Sharon was becoming convinced that something was wrong, Mom had trouble hearing it. It wasn't that she didn't believe Sharon but rather that she didn't want the ugliness spoken out loud, as though acknowledging it would cast it in concrete and set things that way forever.

But my crying on her answering machine had been so hysterical that it had frightened her into action.

That morning, in my bedroom, I was shocked by the reversal of roles. Usually Sharon was angry. Sharon did the talking. Mom was sad and quiet. Mom made excuses for me.

On the drive to my house, Sharon and Mom talked about all of the accounts of my misbehavior. Mom came in pumped up like a boxer after a motivational speech and released all of her fear, concern, anger, and exhaustion as a tirade of accusations that she didn't give me time to answer. Mom is not confrontational and is not very often pushed to anger, but when she gets angry, she gets mean.

"What's wrong with you?" Mom yelled, not as question but as indictment: Something was wrong with me. "What are you doing? Why would you do this?"

Years later, when I was responsible for guiding interventions, I recalled that morning. Mom and Sharon did exactly what I warn people against doing. All drug addicts are different and deal with their addictions and the issues that led them to addiction in different ways, but often, when you accuse a drug addict of doing drugs or having a problem, the natural response is fight or flight. If she flees, she may go out and buy more drugs to help deal with the crisis. If she fights, she may return accusations and shift blame so that she can't hear anything you're saying. Everything Mom and Sharon did was wrong. Yet it was perfect.

"How could you do this to me? How could you do this to Sharon?" Mom yelled.

"Fuck you!" I yelled as a final push to stop her diatribe. I had never spoken to Mom like that. It is alarming to think that I was even capable of saying that to her. You don't speak like that to anybody, especially not to your mother.

That's when Sharon snapped. "How dare you talk to Mommy like that?" she said. "Don't you curse at her. And she's been crying the whole way here. You can't yell at her."

Then Sharon's tone changed. She came at me from the side, rather than head-on. She said, "Can't you see how worried we are? We love you, you know. We want you to be better. We don't want you to die. We want you to be here. Look at what you're doing to Mommy. Stop and look at what you're doing."

Then I did stop.

Mom had curled into herself, sobs shaking her shoulders and sending tears down her cheeks. I looked at Sharon, who seemed less angry than terrified. Until then, I hadn't realized what I was doing to my mother and my sister. When you're in the heat of addiction, when you're in the death grip of it, you truly feel that you are not hurting anybody but yourself. Addicts often say and believe, "I'm not bothering anybody. I'm not doing anything to anyone, so how can I be hurting them?" But when I looked at Mom, and then at Sharon, I could see how injured they were, and I knew that I'd done it to them. That realization shattered the shell inside my skin that I thought had been protecting me but really had been holding me captive. I shrunk back into the bed, hiding in the covers and crying.

But when I looked at Mom, and then at Sharon, I could see how injured they were, and I knew that I'd done it to them. That realization shattered the shell inside my skin that I thought had been protecting me but really had been holding me captive.

Sharon had broken me out of my prison. Sharon is the reason that I got better. She could always see through my lies and would call me on my nonsense. Since my childhood everybody had assumed that I could not care for myself. They had tiptoed around my feelings. They regarded me as fragile and dependent because my parents were divorced, then because I was diagnosed with juvenile diabetes. But Sharon never babied me that way. She wouldn't make excuses for me or accept the excuses I gave her. She expected more. When she spoke to me, she was direct. She said things that were hard to say and hear. She was honest. Because of that, when I was an addict, I was afraid of her.

I knew I wasn't fooling her that day when I yelled that I wanted her and Mom to leave me alone, told her that I was fine, that they were wrong. Sharon knew me. She saw me, and I was beaten.

And saved.

"I need help. Please help me," I cried into my covers. "I can't stop doing cocaine."

The reality of what was happening and who I had become was named, and in naming it, it became real. A real thing could be dealt with, understood, and treated. It became undeniable. That was the most terrifying thing of all.

By acknowledging my problem that day, I made it visible, and visibility made it vulnerable. That day reversed my course. My addiction was no longer hunting me but rather being hunted by me. I felt free. It was such a great relief to finally have Sharon and Mom know the truth: I was in trouble. I was crying. Mom was crying. Sharon was crying.

It was probably the worst day that the three of us have ever had. And also the best day. It was both an end and a beginning, and it held the grief and joy of both.

Mom and Sharon sat on my bed beside me and held me. I repeated over and over, "Please help me." And they did.

They helped me to pack up my things, and I left Tiffany's house and that life behind. I moved to Mom's house. Then onto treatment.

I think now another factor that made the intervention successful that day was the close relationship I had with Mom and Sharon. We were a tight unit. Of course, we had other family—grandparents, our dad, a stepmother, half siblings—but the three of us were something separate and closer than all of that. Together, we were a tight core navigating the world. We were not only in one another's lives; we were one another's lives. Although I had felt alone for so long, Mom and Sharon had been there with me as much as I had allowed them to be. I could not deny their request to be let fully back into my life, no matter what kind of mess my life had become.

CHAPTER THREE
Runaway

Sharon

Sometimes the memories we cling hardest to
are the ones that hurt us the most.
—Elizabeth May, The Falconer

One of my earliest memories is of running away from home. I was three; Lisa was still a baby. My parents were fighting, and I suppose that's why I left. But they were always fighting. They fought over everything—stupid things. They once fought over a cuckoo clock—if it was working, or whose it was, or to what time it should be set. They found things to fight about, and on the day I ran away, they were fighting.

It's hard to imagine now what originally attracted my parents to one another and how they were able to maintain a relationship long enough to marry and have children. They are incredibly different people who ended up living very opposite lives.

They met and married in Israel. Back then they were both Jewish. Mom was born and grew up in Finland and went to study at the University of Tel Aviv for a year when she was eighteen. My dad was also studying in Tel Aviv for a year. They married and stayed in Israel for a few years, until after I was born. When I was three months old, my parents moved our little family to New Jersey, where we first lived in an apartment in Hackensack, then in a house in Teaneck, and eventually moved to Glen Rock. We were living in Teaneck when I ran away.

For a three-year-old, I was fairly well equipped to hit the road on my own. I had traveled a lot with my family—to Finland to see my grandparents, back to Israel, from one house to another. I had my own little suitcase that I packed with survival and travel essentials: a change of clothes, a favorite doll, a box of crayons, a stolen cookie. My parents were preoccupied with their argument as I latched the case closed, carried it down the hallway, and slipped out the door into the peace of the outdoors.

Teaneck is a small town of less than forty thousand people not even an hour from New York City. It borders the lazy Hackensack River with two-story family homes set behind lush, ungated lawns. In the fall people rake their leaves into neat piles; in the winter they shovel the walks of snow; in the summer they mow their lawns in straight rows. At all times of the year, they say hello when they pass neighbors on walks and pick up after their dogs. Even the downtown is friendly and unassuming: quiet brick shops, restaurants, family-owned corner stores, and the ice cream parlor that I frequented as a kid and walked into, suitcase in hand, the day that I ran away.

The thing about running away when you're a kid is that it isn't about going somewhere; it's about leaving. And maybe it isn't really even about that but about attention and being noticed. I was three years old and my parents' attention was on a new baby, work, and the many ways that they could disagree with and blame one another. Eventually they would notice that I was gone. In the meantime I sat at the counter, legs dangling off the edge of the metal stool, suitcase at my feet.

"Are you here all by yourself?" he may have asked. "Do your parents know you're here?"

"I ran away," I might have told him boldly.

Before he ducked into the back to call my mom, he asked me if I wanted a scoop of vanilla or chocolate. Running away was a great deal of work, after all. I wouldn't want to start out hungry.

Mom came to fetch me, and we walked the short distance back to the house together. I remember the police being at our house when we arrived home, but it was as likely a crowd of concerned neighbors and a general chaos stirred up by my inexplicable absence. I also remember standing near the refrigerator and my father hitting the top of it with a particular violence that shuttered through the metal. He had never hit me; he didn't hit me then, but I knew that the impact of his fist with the fridge door was meant for me or was about me—a deep frustration and fear. That image of my father sticks with me. He had puzzling and complex emotions and a general disgust with a world that had gotten out of his control.

* * *

A little over a year later, we moved to Glen Rock, where I had to repeat kindergarten. It feels significant mostly because years later I taught kindergarten and also because it continued to be a joke among my friends through elementary and high school. The repeated year had to do with district cutoff days for admissions: Teaneck accepted younger kindergarteners than Glen Rock.

About the time I was in my second kindergarten year, when Lisa was two and I was five, my dad borrowed $50,000 from Mom's parents to open a liquor and deli store in Teaneck. It was a small neighborhood store that sold liquor on one side and had a deli on the other. The store launched both of my parents' careers in sales. Mom became very successful, and my dad became an award-winning liquor salesman. He was extremely smart and charismatic; he could sell anything to anyone.

But the liquor and deli store in Teaneck also ushered in the end of my parents' marriage. Only a few months after we moved to Glen Rock, they split up. The timing and the move seemed contrived. Glen Rock was right next to the town where my dad's parents lived. He moved our small family close to a support system, stayed long enough to see that we were settled, then disappeared without warning. One day my dad brought Lisa and I to his parents' house, kissed us goodbye as though he were going out to run errands, and did not return for months. When he came back to Glen Rock, he had a beard and a new wife. My dad had met another woman—at work no less: Janet, the "Deli Girl," as Mom called her. Janet and my dad had gone to Las Vegas, somehow managed to get his marriage to Mom annulled, and then married each other.

When my dad came to see Lisa and me, he brought us out to his car where Janet, our new stepmother, was waiting to meet us. She must have already been pregnant with my half brother, Tom.

My dad not only had a new wife, he also had a new religion, having converted from Judaism to Catholicism—Janet 's religion. He had also changed his name to be more Italian-sounding. In the following years, he would continue to invent and revise his identity and his past, becoming a year younger, a former marine, and a dedicated father. Lisa and I often didn't fit into the new image that our father was creating—the children of a failed and abandoned relationship.

* * *

After my parents divorced, Lisa and I lived with Mom. My dad, when he could be convinced to pay, paid a minimal amount of child support. Mom worked hard to keep us in our house in the upper-class town of Glen Rock, often holding two or three jobs at a time. She refused to leave even when her parents encouraged her to move us to Finland where they could be of help or friends encouraged her to move to cheaper neighborhoods.

Mom turned the basement of our house into an efficiency apartment that could be rented for a little extra income, and we had a series of helpful tenants who, along with babysitters, assisted with our care. The first person who lived there was an employee at the liquor deli—that Mom still managed. When she moved out, a man named Al moved in and stayed for years. He was like an uncle to us and often around when Mom was at work.

I would walk home from school with friends to find dinner set out on the stove and a little note of instruction from Mom: "At five-thirty, preheat the oven to three-fifty." The three of us always ate together as a family. As a working mother, I now appreciate how amazing Mom was throughout our childhoods.

Lisa and I were also very close to Mom's parents. Lisa and I flew to Finland alone to see them for the first time when Lisa was five and I was eight. Starting that summer we spent six weeks of our summer vacation with them each year while Mom stayed in New Jersey to work. Like Mom, our grandparents treated us like treasures.

Life at my dad's house was much less stable. He and Janet moved constantly within a small constellation of towns surrounding Glen Rock, fixing up houses and selling them. At Mom's house, Lisa,

Mom, and I were a tight-knit unit. At my dad and Janet's houses, Lisa and I were an addition, along with Janet's children from her previous relationships, who also made visits. At Mom's house Lisa and I had our own bedrooms and her total devotion; at our dad and Janet's houses we slept on a pullout sofa in the living room or on cots in the basement and at best felt extraneous and at worst detested.

Throughout our childhoods Lisa and I spent every other weekend with our dad and Janet, who lived in nearby towns. Janet had left her second marriage to marry my dad and had six children of her own, who primarily lived with her former husband. Like my dad, she often denied her old life, including any responsibilities or relationships to the children of her previous marriage, to fill the vision she had of her new one.

At one point my dad and Janet were living in a town called Wyckoff and refurbishing their house there. Lisa and I visited one weekend, along with Janet's children from her previous marriage. Janet's eldest daughter was on a swing in the backyard when the neighbor came over.

"You have a few more kids this weekend," the neighbor may have said. "Who is that?" she asked, indicating Janet's daughter, who was working to pump the swing higher.

"She's my niece," I overheard my stepmother lie to the neighbor.

An unnamable chill took hold in my toes and chased the scream that started in my chest, catching it in an arrested stare behind my eyes before it could escape from my lips. I suppose that Janet didn't want to explain our complicated family situation to the woman who would only be a neighbor for a matter of months, but also she didn't want to be known as the mother who had abandoned her other children or the woman who had divorced and remarried. Like my dad, Janet had completely reinvented herself. She no longer acknowledged the poor, blue-collar home that she had come from. Now she was educated, sophisticated, proper, and loyal to one family.

Over a decade later, I was at the center of a similar situation when I attended the high school graduation for my half sister, Annie—my dad and Janet 's younger child. Although I was there with my dad and Janet, they did not acknowledge me. I was not introduced to friends or brought in on conversations. Before and after the ceremony, my dad moved in his usual gregarious fashion around the crowd, talking to other parents. He'd pat my half brother, Tom, on the shoulder—everyone knew Tom—and tell whoever would listen what his son was up to. Janet would chime in. I was there beside them, taking up space, using up oxygen, an obstacle that they tripped over. I had this strange sense of being invisible at first, then something much worse: They were ashamed of me.

* * *

I tolerated childhood visits to my dad's house. I never bothered to analyze my feelings or emotions then. It was a routine decided by the adults who had control of my life, and like all such things, it seemed not only set in stone but also as much a part of the stone as its colors or degree of hardness.

I never bothered to analyze my feelings or emotions then. It was a routine decided by the adults who had control of my life, and like all such things, it seemed not only set in stone but also as much a part of the stone as its colors or degree of hardness.

My dad always picked up Lisa and me and dropped us off. In all the years of doing so, he never walked us up to Mom's house or even pulled into the driveway. After he dropped us off, he backed out so that he didn't have to drive past the front entrance. When I was a child, it was another part of our routine. Just a few years ago, when he was visiting me, he told me that he would cry every time he watched us walk away, back up to Mom's door. I believe that. But as a child, I never saw that side of him. He seemed vengeful rather than sad.

Even on the weekends when we were visiting my dad, we didn't really see him. Most of the contact we had with him was during the ride to and from his house. Once we arrived at his house, he would vanish, often into the garage with the excuse of working on something. Mostly Lisa and I played with the other kids: Tom and Annie and Janet's children from her previous marriage, who were close to my age and often there the same weekends. Later, when I was an adult, my dad told me that he and Janet would fight every time Lisa and I were over. He didn't want to deal with Janet, he said, and so he found excuses to leave the house and hide, leaving Lisa and me in Janet's care.

Lisa was much more attentive during those visits. At home, she was the youngest and doted after, lavished with attention. At our dad's house, she was just one of the pack, another whiny voice asking for a snack or wanting attention. Lisa has always been an extrovert, seeking outward connections and validation; I found peace in solitude. I kept to myself. I escaped into books. I played with my dad's German shepherd, Samantha, whom I adored. I was content doing my own thing.

At the end of one weekend, my dad drove us home and parked on the street, hidden from the front door. He drove a VW van, which at the time I thought was cool. He presented well, as though he were always on stage, a spotlight shining on him, a production that was practiced and poised. Before Lisa and I got out of the car, he said there was something he needed to tell us.

"From now on," he said, "when you're at our house and you're talking about your mother, you can no longer say, 'Mommy.' Say, 'My mother. My mother did this.' Don't say, 'Mommy.'"

When we asked why, he said it was because it confused Tom and Annie when we talked about "Mommy." To them, "Mommy" was their mommy.

"Okay," we agreed.

As bizarre as that request was, what stands out to me about that conversation now is the way that he referred to his house as "our house" in a way that so clearly indicated that the "our" meant his, Janet's, Tom's, and Annie's. We—Lisa and I—were not a part of the "our." He never referred to it as "your house." It wasn't for us. It wasn't ours. It was theirs. And in their house, there were no other mommies besides Janet. The same magic trick of rhetoric that had turned our father's Jewish name into something more Catholic sounding and had made of Janet's daughter an innocuous niece would now diminish our dad's previous relationship to something sterile and distant in our mouths. A word nearly foreign to us: mother, my mother. As children, we learned and repeated this language without consideration. As an adult, I see how this limited our roles. We were powerless to act, and also powerless to understand completely the affects the accumulation of these small things had on us: the lack of space set aside for us, the absence of public acknowledgment, the restriction of what we were allowed to say. The message was indirect but definite. We understood it not as something we could name but as something we felt: Our dad did not want us.

CHAPTER FOUR

Fathers and Families

Lisa

Best thing you could probably do as a father is make sure [your kids] see how much you love their mother.
—Matthew McConaughey

I don't remember my parents being married. I can't even imagine them being together. All they had in common was that they were both salespeople—that and their parentage of Sharon and me. What I do remember is my parents being separated and the manifestations of that separation. They were very much like a broken thing—a shattered porcelain cup put back together with old adhesives so that Sharon and I could continue to drink from it. But the shards made for sharp edges that cut our delicate lips, and where the pieces did not fit together, the bowl leaked, spilling the precious nectar—the time, the energy, the attention, the love and care—that we craved.

> What I do remember is my parents being separated and the manifestations of that separation. They were very much like a broken thing—a shattered porcelain cup put back together with old adhesives so that Sharon and I could continue to drink from it.

I should say that it was my dad's house that was broken. Mom made a life of holding Sharon and me tight together and tight to her. She devoted herself to caring for us and letting us know that we were cared for. She made a new and wonderful life and family of the pieces with which my father left her. But I still had this sense, when I was growing up, of an incomplete family and existence.

My understanding of my childhood is retrospective. As an adult I am able to understand my own emotions and actions, although they were a mystery to me at the time. I always knew that Mom loved Sharon and me more than anything in the world, but it was the feeling that my dad did not love me that shaped much of my life. It was not even that I felt unloved by him but rather cast out as someone not worth keeping hold of or even knowing.

Once, when I was a young adult, maybe in my twenties, I returned to Mom's house with Sharon after a visit to our dad's. My grandparents were visiting from Finland. Sharon and I sat down in the living room and talked about our visit. Sharon went through a list of all of the things she didn't like about spending time at Dad's house. She was trying to describe how unwelcome we felt, how difficult it was not to have our own space there, how she felt like she was always on the verge of upsetting Janet, how our dad was never there to spend time with us. She sounded annoyed, but really she was expressing some greater hurt. "I don't know why we even bother trying to have a relationship with him," she said but meant, "I feel like I don't have a father at all."

My grandfather said to her, "Why does that bother you? You and your sister have so much love from us." He couldn't understand how such a hole could still exist in our lives when he and my grandmother and Mom were there to fill it.

"You just don't understand," Sharon said.

He really didn't . A lot of people still don't.

Sharon understood that the circumstance was beyond her control—because she knew that she couldn't change it, she didn't try. But I was sure that I could mend the situation if I could just become who my dad wanted me to be. When I could not change enough to earn his attention, I used alcohol, drugs, and lies to be someone else entirely.

* * *

It was also not until I was an adult that I began to look closely at my dad and analyze what he did and why he did it. This was when I first got sober and was working on forgiveness—both seeking forgiveness and also forgiving those who had hurt me. It was easier to forgive the behavior of others when I could understand it. This often meant examining their pasts and childhoods. I did this when I was trying to forgive my dad.

From talking to my dad and mom, I learned that my dad's parents were at least terrible role models for what parents should be and at most abusive and emotionally neglectful. His father was passive. His mother was angry. She used to beat him and his sister daily for small transgressions. It was not only that she would make my dad sit at the kitchen table all night and stare at food that he refused to eat but also that he felt she purposefully prepared things for dinner that she knew he hated and then took pleasure in watching him suffer.

Years ago a relative of mine from California named Adam, whom I'd never met, contacted me. He had been studying the family for twenty years and knew things about my dad's childhood family. He described my dad's mother as a tiny, petite woman and terrible alcoholic. "That woman was the devil," Adam told me.

My dad once said that his mother pushed him down the stairs and his father pretended it didn't happen. I imagine my dad as a little boy, vulnerable and helpless. I imagine him sitting at the dinner table with a bad taste in his mouth and a plate set out before him. I imagine his mother—this small woman with a scream that overwhelmed the entire house. She called him names. She hit him. She threw food in his face. I imagine him crying silently, tears streaking his little face, his hair wet with sweat, his hands trembling in his lap or shaking as they gripped a fork and knife. Then she left the kitchen, and the room went dark. In the other room, sitting in a chair and reading a paper, was his father who, when it was late, walked past the dark kitchen, up the stairs, and to bed, not bothering to check on his young son, who was falling asleep with his chin dipped down on his chest. How alone my dad must have felt. How unloved. How disregarded.

My dad's mother died when he was a kid. My dad had long since stopped talking to his father, but Mom made sure that Sharon and I had a relationship—at least a tentative one—with that side of the family. Once when we were visiting, Mom asked our grandfather why he didn't have any pictures of me and Sharon out in his house. His house was filled with framed photos of his new wife's two children and all of their kids—her grandkids—posed in school photos and with sports teams, but there was no trace of me and Sharon. When my grandfather responded with a dismissive shrug, Mom scolded him. "Shame on you," she said.

My dad left home when he was a teenager. After that point his story becomes ambiguous, a blur of truth and lies, embellished stories alongside invented tales. I don't know what really happened, but I was told—by Mom, and him, and others—that he hitchhiked to Florida and, when he was eighteen, joined the navy—although he tells everyone that he joined the marines. According to Mom, he ended up leaving the navy because he was extremely claustrophobic and couldn't cope in a submarine.

After he left the navy, he went to Israel, where he met Mom. By the time my parents met, my dad had already contrived a better history for himself than that of a terrified child trapped in solitary confinement at a cold dinner table. His new self was charismatic and handsome. He was the life of the party. He could own a room the instant he walked into it. Everyone liked him. He was always in a crowd.

Only upon a closer look would anyone notice that he had many acquaintances but no close friends. My dad is one of those people who is truly unknowable and also one of those people who, even when surrounded by others, is completely alone.

* * *

In my first memories of my parents, they were divorced, my dad was already remarried to my stepmother, Janet, and my half brother, Tom, was on the way. Janet had always been cold in an inconspicuous way. She never confronted Sharon and me directly. Instead she went through my dad, making of him a dummy that spoke to us on her behalf. "Janet doesn't want you to … " "Janet would appreciate it if you would …" "Janet will no longer allow you to … ."

Once, when Sharon and I were about five and eight, I didn't like the sandwich that Janet had made me for lunch. At home Mom would have replaced it or more likely would have known my tastes in the first place. Here, in my dad and Janet's house, I was afraid to say anything. I ate what I could bear to and threw out the rest. Later, my dad pulled me aside. "You can't throw your food away," he scolded. "That was wrong and disrespectful. Janet worked hard to make you lunch. Don't ever do that again." Janet had told on me.

Around that same time, Sharon and I decided to color pictures for Janet. We spent the afternoon with a box of crayons filling in the coloring book pages. I imagined Janet would be delighted. I thought she might put the pictures up on the fridge. But when we presented them to her, she looked them over quickly then handed them back. "I don't want these," she said and walked away.

This incident warranted another talk with our dad. "How could you be so inconsiderate?" he said. One of the pictures was from *Snow White*, a story that featured a wicked stepmother. "Why did you choose that picture? What are you saying about Janet? Why would you hurt her like that?" Even as he scolded us, I couldn't comprehend why he was angry or how we had offended Janet. I couldn't grasp the concept of a stepmother yet and certainly didn't make a connection between Janet and the character in *Snow White*.

As we got older, Janet continued to wait for us to breach the fragile protocols of her house. When I was nine or ten years old, I was talking with Sharon and Maggie, our stepsister from Janet's previous marriage, who was about the same age as Sharon. Sharon and Maggie were talking about sex in the way that thirteen- and fourteen-year-olds do. I didn't know what sex was, and they were trying to explain it to me—what a man does, and what a woman does. We were laughing. It sounded ridiculous. The more they explained, the more we laughed. Then I stopped as if a light bulb had come on over my head in a cartoon and said, "Wait, that means Mommy and Daddy had sex?" It was not only a realization that sex had needed to occur to bring me into the world but also the first time that I really imagined my parents as people who could be in a room together, people who loved one another. I had never thought of them occupying the same space, even just sitting across from one another at a dinner table. I said, "Wait, Mommy and Daddy had sex? That's how I was born?"

Then, from the other room, I heard a gruff "Lisa, come in here right now."

My dad and Janet were in the living room. They were irate. "What are you talking about? You shouldn't be talking about that. That's disgusting. You're disgusting. How dare you talk like that in our house?" They scolded me until I cried. I felt awful and dirty and bad.

I think now that they weren't really upset that I was talking about sex. Really, Janet was offended to hear any mention of Mom or my dad's relationship with Mom. Janet couldn't handle it. And because she couldn't handle it, she took an afternoon of laughter and discovery and turned it into something terrifying and shameful.

* * *

As kids, Sharon and I planned to run away a lot. At Mom's house we did this as a way of pretending to be on an adventure. At my dad's house, we did this as a dream of escape. Sometimes we went so far as to pack suitcases or to imagine what we would pack into suitcases. Even when we were not planning to run away, I often dreamed that I was in some other family, one that was complete and where everyone completely loved me.

Growing up, my dad had a best friend named Jim whom he stayed in touch with into adulthood. After my parents divorced, my dad stopped talking to everyone from his previous life, including his own parents, Jim, and Jim's wife—my dad's high school friend—Grace. Grace and Mom became best friends, and we are all still close. Jim and Grace have three sons around the same ages as Sharon and me. I loved their family when I was young. I loved their house. I loved being around them. Everything felt good there. Everyone liked everyone else. I wanted my family to be that family. I wanted us all to feel that way all of the time. When I dreamed about running away, I dreamed of running there.

When I was an adult, Jim told me that when my dad was a teenager, he had run away a few times before he had left home for good. "Then he would often run to my house," Jim said. As an adult I spoke to Jim about my dad and my childhood. "I know this might upset you," Jim said, "but you sound just like your father. You sound like your father talking about his house and his father."

I understand that we model behavior unconsciously. But I also know that it is possible to transcend your past, consider how your behavior affects others, and end abusive cycles.

I realize now how much people's behaviors are affected by their past experiences. I understand that we model behavior unconsciously. But I also know that it is possible to transcend your past, consider how your behavior affects others, and end abusive cycles. My dad and Janet had their own trauma to deal with, but they had an opportunity to stop that trauma by treating me and

Sharon better than they had been treated. They didn't make a choice to do that.

I have a few memories of Janet being very loving toward me. One was when I was three and Janet was pregnant with Tom. I was sitting on her lap in the car, pressed against her pregnant belly. My dad was driving me and Sharon home after a weekend visit. Janet was holding me close and playing with my hair. She seemed to genuinely have affection for me, to love me. For years that memory and that feeling of being loved by her really stood out to me.

Years later, after I was in recovery, I recalled that memory again in hypnosis. Then I remembered the following scene, when I left my dad and Janet's car and ran up my sidewalk to Mom, who was waiting at the front door. There was pain in Mom's face. I don't know why Janet loved me in that moment, if it was because she was pregnant and imagining that I was her coming child or if she let her guard down for a moment. I don't know why Mom was so sad, if it was because the divorce was fresh or if it was because she sensed I'd made a connection with my dad's new wife. What I knew for certain in that moment was that love is not kind. Love is complicated and administers pain in the same dosage at which it administers joy.

CHAPTER FIVE
Quitter

Sharon

Life is tough my darling, but so are you.
—Stephanie Bennett Henry

My mother's experience of motherhood was completely different than mine. She was in survival mode through much of it. Motherhood for her lacked a lot of the joy and fret that I allow myself to feel on a daily basis. A few months ago, my oldest son, Joe, started college. My husband and I loaded up the car and drove him out of state. We descended upon his new domain—campus, dorm, cafeteria, surrounding town—with the dual purpose of inspecting and absorbing every detail so that we could understand the stories that he would tell us the following year. Like his personal Sherpas, we carried boxes to his room, made trips to local stores to gather the few essentials we'd forgotten, and followed him around campus taking pictures. I had our next visit scheduled before we left. I told him over and over, "You can always come home" and "You know I'm going to miss you" and meant it. He'd warned me not to cry, and I held it together until I was back in the car with Anthony.

My mom was matter-of-fact about Joe leaving home. She didn't seem to understand my concerns about him being out in the world on his own, the way that it would change our little family at home, or the emotional contradiction of feeling excited about his future while mourning the past.

"Oh, he's so close," Mom said easily. "You know what he's up to. Everything is fine."

"Weren't you upset at all when I went away to college?" I asked her.

"I was," she said, "but my life was so different. It was just responsibility after responsibility." Then she said, "For such a long time, I had just wanted someone to take care of me."

She had been relieved in some way when I left home: one less thing to be responsible for, one less thing to worry about. Motherhood for my mom was doing what was necessary to take care of the most pressing issues then doing what was necessary to take care of the next issue to arise. She did not have the energy to think beyond the chaos of the present moment—to plan our next visit, wonder if our semesters would be better if we changed classes, or mourn the loss of our presence at the breakfast table. She never wavered in the face of her duty to take care of the trials that mounted in front of her. She never considered neglecting what was necessary to keep us safe and well. She made of each challenge a step-by-step to-do list that, if followed, would lead her to accomplish the task. She could not let herself be distracted by the details that I lavish in.

While my life is different, I am so much like Mom. I am practical and orderly. I see a task in front of me, understand the goal at the end, find a path between the two, and barrel through. But for Mom motherhood was often limited to that: a task. I am not spread as thin. For me there is time to enjoy each moment, to miss my eldest, and even to continue to worry and feel responsible for him although he is an adult and living away from home.

* * *

Our mom's life only become more complicated by the fact that Lisa was diagnosed with juvenile diabetes. She was six. For me, being in the fourth grade, the diagnosis felt sudden—we were in our usual routine of school, work, and home, and then one day Lisa was in the hospital.

But Mom had been noticing the symptoms for months and would spend many more years using so much of her mental energy monitoring and tracking the ways these symptoms manifested in Lisa. At my grandfather's wedding—my father's father, who was getting married for the third time months after my step-grandmother had passed away—Mom watched my sister drink cup after cup of Coke. Lisa was peeing at the same rate that she was drinking. She was on a relay race, running to Mom to ask for a drink, then racing back to Mom to be escorted to the bathroom. Mom had a cousin who was diabetic and realized that something was wrong.

When Mom brought Lisa to the hospital, Lisa's blood sugar level was dangerously high. The doctors admitted her immediately.

The process of getting Lisa diagnosed and starting her treatment was one of those rare times when Mom and my dad had to be present in the same space. These occurrences were always uncomfortable. They would say brief, obligatory hellos and then avoid eye contact for the rest of the event, slipping into other rooms to separate themselves. Neither of them knew how to relax when the other was around or how to make their togetherness easy for everyone else. Mom often busied herself with the business at hand, and my dad, on the other hand, retreated. It was my dad's tendency to spend time feeling sorry for himself—even when having a child admitted to the hospital or celebrated in a school ceremony—to make the moment about himself.

For all my dad's faults, he really got on board with Lisa's diabetic treatment. While she was in the hospital, everyone had to be taught about testing blood—done with a finger prick—and giving shots, including Lisa, who, at six years old, would mostly be responsible for administering her own insulin.

After Lisa was released from the hospital, there was a new focus on food at both Mom's and our dad's houses. At both houses we had always eaten dinner together, but now mealtimes were on a strict schedule, sweets were limited and, mostly, there was a conscious observation of Lisa—everyone on the lookout for signs (shifts in mood and energy levels) that her blood sugar may be low or high.

After her diagnosis, Lisa's diabetes not only hung in the air, but became the very air that we all breathed. Everything was about Lisa, who was not only in need of extra care but also as cute as a button. I was jealous. I started pretending to be sick. I would complain of vague symptoms and nestle into Mom's hip, wanting the same cautious regard and soothing caress that she gave Lisa. She obliged when she was able and otherwise said things like, "Are you really feeling bad?" I of course now have a mother's understanding of why Lisa needed so much attention—her health simply demanded it. But even if I knew this as a child, it didn't change the jealously and resentment I felt watching Lisa be the one on the receiving end of all of our mother's care.

It didn't help either that around this time I started to regard Lisa as a liar. She lied all of the time. After her diagnosis, she started to lie about food. Ironically, a year after Lisa was diagnosed, Mom started working as a salesperson for a candy company. She would come home in the evenings with a car full of jawbreakers, lollypops, and gummy bears. Lisa would sneak them out of the trunk then deny that she had done it. But it wasn't only that. She would make up stories for no reason, say that she'd done things she hadn't, lie about where she'd been or where she was going. Her lying was so relentless that I assumed that anything she said was fabricated.

Mostly, I did not report Lisa's misdeeds and lies, although I always knew what Lisa was up to. My stance was one of passive observer: There's my annoying little sister sneaking around again. It wasn't until I had my own family that I began to look at my role in situations differently. Once I had children, I could no longer ignore bad behavior. It was then that my relationships with my childhood family began to change.

Mom never wanted to believe that Lisa would intentionally do anything wrong and had a process for dealing with such claims when I did make them: First she would ignore hints of Lisa's bad behavior, then she would deny that Lisa could have engaged in misconduct and offer alternative culprits; when Lisa's involvement was undeniable, Mom offered excuses for Lisa's behavior, her go-to reason being that "her blood sugar was probably low." Lisa's diabetes had become her get-out-of-jail-free card.

In Mom's defense, when we were children, her focus was so squarely on Lisa's health that she had no energy to focus on Lisa's behavior. Being a single mother had already been difficult; now she was the single mother of a child with special health needs.

My teacher at the time saw the toll these changes in our family dynamic had on me. She would direct a strange, close notice on me that was both sympathetic and wary. She gave me sad looks and couldn't keep herself from continually trying to fix the bangs that hung in my face because I was trying to them grow out. It was as though she saw my awkward hairstyle, contemplative silences, even my laughter with friends as signs that I was being neglected at home. I still think about that teacher now that I am a teacher myself and at times see what could be evidence of trouble at home in the behaviors or appearances of my students. Yet I am quite certain I was not being neglected in any way back then. Other teachers understood my situation and rallied in more supportive ways. They saw Mom raising Lisa and me on her own, Lisa sick, and me falling into the background, and offered us what they could. My teachers were truly amazing.

* * *

A lot of what I learned from childhood—maybe in great part because of Lisa's diagnosis—was to fend for and count on myself. As much as Mom and Lisa were in my life, and as supportive as my teachers were, I was really on my own. Because I wasn't sick, and was not only older but also capable and responsible, people around me assumed that I didn't need help. I could cope, I could figure things out, and I could be trusted. For me that meant that I learned to be independent and also not to ask for help or expect anyone to lend a hand or offer guidance.

It also meant that no one pushed me to challenge myself or monitored my progress. I set my own standards and goals. I often set the bar low—something easy and definitely attainable. I only attempted what I believed I could do, and in many cases I didn't believe I could do much. When something was difficult, I retreated. I quit everything. No one held me accountable. I hear myself saying to my own children now, “You committed to the team, play for the season” or “We invested money in those lessons, keep practicing.” I acknowledge that the things that my children are doing may be difficult or uncomfortable, but I also know it is important to work through those frustrations. I want them to be successful and to have the confidence to know they can be successful. No one encouraged me in that way. I quit Brownies, soccer, dance, clubs, and jobs. I quit everything that I started all through elementary school, junior high, high school, and my first year of college. I quit because I wasn’t immediately good at it, or because some aspect of it was awkward, because it was too much work, or annoying, or I didn’t like the schedule, because it wasn’t what I had expected, or I just didn’t see the point. I would come home and announce to Mom that I wanted to quit something. Mom would nod and say, “Okay.”

I acknowledge that the things that my children are doing may be difficult or uncomfortable, but I also know it is important to work through those frustrations. I want them to be successful and to have the confidence to know they can be successful.

That would be that.

Mom didn’t have time to be my cheerleader. And I seemed strong enough to stand on my own. She needed to attend to Lisa, the mortgage, housekeeping, and other stuff of life. Our family was a house of cards built by Mom’s careful and practiced hand. If she let herself be distracted, it would collapse. It would have been a struggle to convince or discipline me. And I seemed fine without Brownies, soccer, dance, clubs, and the rest of it. These things individually were not essential, but those little decisions formed a larger pattern.

Something changed for me in college. I was a freshman at Ohio State University. I'd been excited about going, but in the middle of the fall semester, I felt homesick and I decided to quit. "Okay," Mom said. "Rent a truck and come home."

It was December, and I was just about to turn nineteen. I packed my room, loaded everything into a U-Haul, and drove home to New Jersey from Ohio alone. I didn't consciously think it then, but that had sort of been my life in a nutshell. No one was going to make me stay. No one was going to help me leave. It was up to me to make a decision and make the decision work.

Maybe it was because quitting was so difficult that time, or because maturity allowed me to look at things more objectively, or because I was thinking of my future and whether I wanted to go on that way—quitting everything—but at that point I decided to make a change. After Ohio State, I never quit anything again. It's a joke in my house now. My kids know that they cannot be like I was. They can never quit.

I have maintained this fierce sense of independence and determination ever since. Even now I am sometimes independent and self-reliant to ridiculous levels. I broke my arm a couple of years ago and took myself to the hospital. It happened late at night when everyone in my house was sleeping. Rather than wake my husband, which now seems the sane solution, I made a sling of my jacket sleeve, put myself in the car, drove one-handed to the hospital, and checked myself into the emergency room. X-rays done, cast in place, I drove myself home, crawled into bed, and woke the next morning to explain everything to my family at the breakfast table. I realized later that nobody ever offered to help me with anything that entire evening: not to open a door or hold the paper as I signed or free my insurance card from my wallet. I acknowledge that with a sense of pride but also a trace of grief. It is devastating not to be offered help. I know this is in great part my own fault: I look capable; I look like I'm in control; I put off an air that tells people, "Stay out of my way and let me take care of things." Independence is freeing and also isolating.

It is devastating not to be offered help. I know this is in great part my own fault: I look capable; I look like I'm in control; I put off an air that tells people, "Stay out of my way and let me take care of things." Independence is freeing and also isolating.

People often tell me that they admire how capable I am. They regard me as like Samantha from *Bewitched*, this otherworldly woman who sees trouble about to happen, calmly decides upon a solution, and twitches her nose to magically make things right. I have mastered the illusion of doing what I do in ways that make it seem effortless. No one realizes that I am working to near exhaustion all day long.

I sometimes complain to my husband about having too much responsibility. "I would just like somebody besides me to take care of it."

He knows that in the end I will do everything myself and refuse any help offered. "Things are this way because you make them this way. You want to be in control. You're never happy with things when someone else does them for you."

"I know," I say, but one day I'd like to not have to do it.

It isn't that I don't know any other way to be. I see people asking for help. I understand humble dependence. There are people around me whom I adore who never lift a finger to do anything for themselves. They see how allowing people to serve them gives those other people pleasure. But letting people wait on me in that way would make me come out of my skin. I'm not comfortable being any other way. Independence and self-reliance are ingrained in me. I am the strong one, the capable one, the one who is always fine on her own.

CHAPTER SIX
Liar, Liar

Lisa

Our anxiety does not come from thinking about
the future, but wanting to control it.
—Kahlil Gibran

As a child and young adult, I had trouble dealing with, or even knowing, my true emotions. This was shaped by a couple of things. The first was that I have always been very empathetic. I not only perceive the emotions of others but also often occupy them in a personal way, feeling the sadness, anger, or frustration of other people as though their emotions were my own. I remember once when I was young, I was in the car with Mom, and we stopped at a red light. I looked out the window into the car next to us. An elderly man sat alone behind the wheel. My face dropped to near tears. "What's wrong?" Mom asked.

"I'm so sad because he's alone," I said.

"I can't believe you're saying that," Mom said to me. "You're so little."

I was a strange soul.

My extreme empathy meant that I often confused the feelings of other people with my own and also that I felt deep sympathy for other people, even strangers. I was constantly working to mediate the emotions around me. I felt responsible in some way for other people's happiness because I could sense their sadness. This led to the other issue that disconnected me from my own feelings: I had a desire to appear happy no matter how I really felt. My desire was so strong that I split myself into two, the core of my being separating from the surface. On the surface I not only appeared happy but also accepted the situation and found contentment in that way that children do, no matter the circumstance. The problem was that on a deeper level, I was dying. I couldn't acknowledge or even identify my negative emotions. Even when things were sad, I would laugh.

I felt responsible in some way for other people's happiness because I could sense their sadness. This led to the other issue that disconnected me from my own feelings: I had a desire to appear happy no matter how I really felt.

When I was a junior in high school, a close friend of mine died in a car accident. I knew that I was supposed to cry, but I couldn't access my feelings. I didn't cry until her funeral, when my tears were as much a social response to the hysterical crying of my other friends and our parents. It was a strange feeling of being distant from myself.

I think that this is why my memories of being in the hospital when I was diagnosed with diabetes are mostly happy. I was admitted in November of 1980, one month before I turned seven. I have a picture of myself in the hospital from that time, standing in front of the large windows in my room. I am wearing a light pink flowered nightgown with childish elastic ruffles at the ends of the sleeves that have been pushed lazily up my arms. In front of me, I am holding a large teddy bear, half my size and dressed in a dapper long sleeved black shirt and green bow. The bear has the stubby, jointless arms of a toddler, stretched upward, as though he is reaching to be picked up. I am smiling with my entire face as I hug his soft body to mine. On my wrist there is a hospital band. While I hold the bear—my arms wrapped around him, my hands folded one over the other—the fingers of one hand reach to touch that strange plastic band on the other. It is so imperceptibly loose and light, yet there to be pulled and twisted. On it, it says things that I can read already (my name, my date of birth) and other things about my condition that I cannot read.

In the hospital I was surrounded by people who loved me and given attention by family and doctors alike. Even my dad and step-mother seemed, in that moment, to genuinely care for me. They came to visit me one day, and I proudly offered to give them a tour of the hospital—I had become quite familiar with the terrain. I held both of their hands and walked both between and in front of them, pulling them along the brightly lit hallways lined with railings and doors to all of the places I knew: the nurses station, lobby, water fountain, vending machine. It was the first time that I had ever been alone with them, without Sharon or Mom or any half siblings. I had their undivided attention. "My, you've made a lot of friends," they said as I waved to a familiar nurse down the hall.

For days I had been taking visitors as though I were hosting an extended slumber party. One day my entire first grade class came to see me, crowding my room. I showed them how the hospital bed went up and down, how I could press a button and call a nurse, how I had control of the remote that changed the channels of the wall-mounted television. I showed them the band on my wrist. It was all very exciting. Although I know now that I must have felt tired and sick, my memory is not of feeling physically ill but rather feeling emotionally content. The surface of my being was pleased to be embraced by people who cared about me.

There were other times that I do remember feeling incredibly sick. I frequently came down with stomach viruses when I was in elementary school. I would have such sharp pains that I would sit next to the toilet and scream and then plead with Mom, "Why does God hate me? Why is he doing this to me?" It was exhausting, relentless pain that made me clench my teeth and shake. It filled each breath and stopped time for long intervals. It truly felt like I was being punished. I was too little to understand that it would ever end.

But in the hospital, I do not remember feeling pain or even feeling sick. On the tour I gave to my dad and Janet, I eventually released their hands and skipped down the hall ahead of them in my nightgown and socks. I sang and waved to people in rooms whom I didn't know, then circled back to find my dad and Janet's hands again.

In the months previous, Mom had grown increasingly worried about me. I had been losing weight, wetting the bed, drinking too much, and complaining of strange pains and cravings. During those months I had seen this particular expression of concern in her face—an expression that would continue to appear throughout my childhood, adolescence, and troubled early adult life.

The definition of the diagnosis seemed to put her at ease to some degree. Once the doctors got my blood sugar under control, they began working on teaching me how to handle my diabetes. They brought me a tray of oranges and a syringe, and I practiced giving the fruit shots of saline.

The first months after I returned home, my parents took responsibility for giving me shots. Shockingly, it was my dad who taught me how to give myself injections. It was a strange time in our relationship, one during which he was gentle and patient with me. He would carefully pinch what little fat there was on my arms or legs and say, "Like this," push the needle in, then take it out. "You try."

I don't know if it was because the situation was so serious, or because the interaction that I needed was so defined, or because Janet for some reason encouraged rather than discouraged his engagement with me, but those memories of him helping me stand out as significant

Momentarily my diabetes seemed to bring out the best in the people around me. Even my parents were in better communication with one another. That summer they decided together that I should go to Camp Nejeda, an overnight camp for kids with diabetes. There, in addition to the swimming, sports, crafts, hikes, and play, there was also rigorous tracking of every meal served, lessons on how to test blood and give insulin shots, and open discussions about what it was like to live with diabetes.

* * *

It was difficult to be a kid with diabetes—an illness that demanded an adult sense of responsibility. I don't think that I really lied more or in different ways than other kids, but my lies had bigger consequences because of my illness. I had a blood testing kit at home that I was supposed to use regularly to test my blood sugar. Mom had bought me a journal to keep track of my blood test scores, food, and notes about how I was feeling. I spent hours decorating and making it special. Every day I opened it and wrote things. Most important was the record of my blood sugar levels, but I had long since stopped pricking my finger and drawing blood to conduct the test. Like a child who does not really brush her teeth, but only runs the toothbrush under the water to give evidence to her fib, I memorized the acceptable range for my blood sugar and wrote a number that only slightly varied from the number I had written the previous day. It seemed harmless. I didn't want to prick my finger and examine my blood, but I wanted Mom to be proud of my independence. It seemed like the perfect solution. For a long while, it worked, or seemed to work.

But my blood sugar was constantly getting dangerously low. I would go pale, become listless and disoriented. "Lisa, are you all right? Are you all right?" Mom would cry in a panic before she would decide that I was entirely not all right and call for an ambulance. The paramedics would give me a shot of glucose, load me onto the gurney, and take me to the hospital. It became routine.

Eventually my forged testing was discovered. Mom was disappointed and worried. I felt guilty and ashamed.

Many things about being diabetic were demoralizing for me as a child. I didn't like the way that it controlled my life and became who I was rather than something I dealt with. I always had to think about food, to keep track of when and what I ate. "Every two hours" became a mantra. In school I was pulled out of class daily for years and made to eat a snack. It made me different in a terrible way.

Diabetes also became a ready excuse for everything, first used by adults, then appropriated by me: Why hadn't I completed my homework? My blood sugar had been low; Why was I late? I'd had an issue with my insulin; Why hadn't I done my chores? I wasn't feeling well. No one ever questioned me when I offered an excuse related to my illness. My desires and strategies weren't that different from those of my peers, but my diabetes offered a reliable support to any white lie that would get me out of things that I didn't want to do.

I remember the first time that I really lied intentionally. I was around eight years old, and a teacher asked me if I had taken a piece of candy. I looked her in the eye and said no, as though that was the most ridiculous idea.

I snuck sweets all the time, although I knew that I shouldn't have them. I ate them in secret, hidden away under a bed or in a closet. It was a foreshadowing of what was to come, practice for larger betrayals and abuses to my own body. That lie was also practice for my later life, the blatant fib that protected me from getting into trouble. Not only did lying make me feel awful, but it also brought the fear of being caught: Now I would not only be in trouble for stealing the candy but also for not telling the truth.

White lies about my diabetes—often told to teachers and authority figures—afforded me the freedom to get and do what I wanted. I would tell my teachers that my blood sugar was low, and they would release me into the hallway to go and see the nurse, where I would just rest on a cot while the rest of my classmates worked on math equations and listened to lectures.

And in that way, I was screwed by the disease at eight years old, when I first learned that lying was a working strategy for getting out of trouble and creating opportunities. I graduated from using white lies to get out of class to telling boldface lies to hide my drug addiction. By the time I discovered cocaine in my late twenties, I was an expert at hiding things, misleading people, covering bad behavior, and misdirecting attention. With all those lies always came the anxiety that I would be caught and the shame that exposure would bring.

Sharon could always see through me. When we were kids, and then adults, I was most afraid of her. I knew that she could tell when I was lying. My regard for her was a kind of reverence. I idolized her.

I was also a very imaginative child engaged in a fantasy life—something I had in common with my dad. It was communally acceptable in my family to confirm the lies that my dad told about his past; it didn't seem much of a stretch to add a few more details. I made up stories about places I'd been and things I'd done. I made up more stories about my dad, who was rarely around to prove me wrong, transforming him into an ideal father, devoted to me. In my fictional life, I could be whoever I wanted to be.

When planning to write this book, I was talking with a friend about the lie that my life had been, and the lie that my dad's life had been. "Even Sharon pretended to be Italian for our dad," I told my friend, who knew my family well.

"Wow, even Sharon did that?" my friend asked. She was shocked.

Sharon always—even as a child—seemed beyond such petty games. She was too honorable and practical and responsible to be caught up in nonsense. She never gave credence to my excuses. She had compassion for my situation but also demanded a kind of integrity from me that other people didn't seem to think I was capable of.

What I got from other people was often pity. I deserved their sympathy. I had to take shots every day. I had to count and consider everything I ate. I was frequently rushed to the hospital. It was awful. Whatever trouble I had caused, I had already endured a punishment for—I was dealing with something I was too young to have to deal with. I knew that the adults in my life felt sorry for me and sorry that they couldn't take my illness away. I genuinely needed the care and concern of others. The problem was that I also preyed upon it; I took advantage of that pity. Moreover, I enjoyed taking advantage—the way that that feeling made me both content and complete and how natural it became to play on the sympathies of others with the stories I told them. I was not addicted to a substance at that point, but it was the start of my addict behavior. I was no longer just lying but also living a lie.

I genuinely needed the care and concern of others. The problem was that I also preyed upon it; I took advantage of that pity.

* * *

Lying was not the only seed that I began nurturing as a young child. A particular kind of despair also began growing deep within me, asserting that I was not worthy of love and attention and that I did not belong anywhere. I always felt different from everyone around me. I felt that I didn't fit in. Throughout childhood I had a lot of friends. I was surrounded by people and invited to do things, but still I felt so very alone. Rejected. Left out. I wanted to get outside of myself, to be someone or somewhere else, or at least to be distant from my own thoughts. Some of that may have been an inclination that was born with me, but a lot of it had to do with my dad, the family he had made with Janet, and the ways they made me feel like I wasn't wanted in their lives.

The last time that I ever spent a weekend at my dad and Janet's house was sometime around my bat mitzvah, when I was thirteen years old. There wasn't particular reason that I stopped engaging in the regular routine of biweekly visits to their house. I was a teenager, and my life had become complicated with social outings, school, sports, and activities. Going to my dad and Janet's house made participation in things difficult. I still saw them on occasion.

When I was fifteen, they moved to Chicago. I didn't see my dad for a year after that. They moved back to New Jersey when I was in high school. The first time that Sharon and I went to visit them afterward, Janet looked at me and said, "My, you're so big."

I was probably ten or fifteen pounds overweight then. In hindsight it isn't even that much, but the women in my family are thin and gorgeous. Mom is fine-boned and has maintained her delicate figure throughout her life. Sharon was always thin and beautiful, like Mom. They could both eat whatever they wanted and never gain a pound.

I remember that when I was first diagnosed with juvenile diabetes, my grandmother—my dad's stepmother—said, "I feel sorry for you." She had not meant that she felt sorry that I was sick, or that I would have to take shots, or keep track of my food, or eat every two hours, or have times of high and low blood sugar that would require trips to the hospital; she had instead meant that she felt sorry that I would lose my figure.

In the eighties, before the insulin pump was available, the treatment of diabetes was a guessing game. Diabetics would test their blood sugar, estimate the amount of insulin they would need in accordance with what they planned to eat, take a shot, wait an hour, then eat a meal. After a meal, if their blood sugar was high, they might take more insulin; if it was low, they might eat again. My blood sugar would frequently be low, and I would feel hungry. I often ended up eating two dinners.

"Lisa got so big!" Janet kept saying to my father. She would often do that, speak about us right in front of us. I was sixteen, an adolescent girl self-conscious and embarrassed of my body. "Look at her. What happened? I can't believe how big she's gotten."

I went home and told Mom, "I don't ever want to go there again." I said.

Mom, usually the diplomat who encouraged me and Sharon to be forgiving and kind and directed us to maintain civilities—including visits with my dad and Janet—agreed that I should not have to go back.

"Fine," she said. "No problem."

That was the last overnight visit I had with my dad and Janet.

CHAPTER SEVEN

Merry Christmas

Sharon

You can't avoid hurt. Your only choice is to live through it.
—Rebekah Crane, The Upside of Falling Down

It took me five years and three colleges to complete a BS degree in education—credits lost to transferring cost me a few extra semesters. Two and a half of those years I spent at home, living at first with Mom and Lisa while Lisa was still in high school, then later living alone with Mom after Lisa had moved out. The basement apartment that Mom had rented out when Lisa and I were kids was vacant, and I moved into the space that was separate from and different than my childhood bedroom.

Lisa was a sophomore the year that I came home—defeated in some way—from Ohio State University and first lived at home and attended community college in town. Although our visits were far and few between, we still saw our dad, who had been back from Chicago for a couple of years. Some contact was obligatory, especially at the holidays, when families were expected—by tradition and family photo albums—to spend time together. At that point it was easier to maintain and go along than it would have been to question and refuse.

And I was not like Lisa, who yearned for something intangible and emotional from our dad. She craved not only connection but also his approval. She wanted him to care about her, and his unwillingness or inability to do so wounded her deeply. For me, interaction with my dad was not hurtful so much as it was inconvenient and irritating. Because our dad never showed signs of lavishing Lisa and me with attention or affection, wanting such attention seemed futile. I tolerated a visit or two a year—hours lost from my life. When I saw my dad as I got older, I was often purposefully aloof. I was there not to catch up with him but to be seen by him. I showed off. I wanted him to know how well I was doing despite his disregard.

I had also learned that while our dad could not be counted on for emotional connection, he was sometimes good for material gifts. I used his sense of fatherly duty and guilt for not fulfilling that duty to capitalize on what he had to offer: used cars, radios, occasional cash. His absence also meant that I could make up stories about him to impress friends—they would never have had any way of finding out the truth.

The distance between me and my dad got wider as I became a young adult. I always dreaded talking to him on the rare occasions when he called. Our conversations were the curt, polite question and answer of strangers making small talk in grocery store lines, often alternating with long, awkward silences. It wasn't that we didn't know how to talk to one another but rather that neither of us had anything to say. It felt as though we were putting our time in, punching a clock at one of the many minimum wage jobs I was working then, recording that we had made an effort to communicate, although no meaningful exchange ever happened between us. He wasn't interested in what I was doing. I wasn't interested in his life either. Eventually I stopped answering the phone. He called less. That thin but steady stream between us became only a trickle, and then a line drawn in the dirt. Finally, I stopped talking to him altogether.

My dad maintained his adopted Catholic identity, so while Lisa and I were occupied at Jewish holidays with Mom and, oddly enough, our dad's parents—with whom he no longer had ties—we spent Catholic holidays with our dad and our stepmother, Janet.

I was nineteen and Lisa was sixteen the last time we went to Christmas at my dad and Janet's house. Lisa and I had been old enough for a few years not to need to be picked up by our dad, which meant that we had the space of the drives from one New Jersey town to another to talk, prepare, and psych ourselves up for the visit. That last year we went, we guessed as we drove what odd things Janet might say to us, what looks we might get from our dad, how our half brother and half sister, Tom and Annie—only a couple years younger than Lisa—would have changed since we had last seen them. Mostly, we avoided talking about our dad's house. We talked about my months at Ohio State University and how the high school in Glen Rock had changed in the three years since I'd been a sophomore—as Lisa was then. We talked about the news, the weather, bands that we'd discovered, boyfriends. We talked about Mom. We talked about the previous evening, Christmas Eve, which we always spent sleeping over at friends' houses since we didn't celebrate the holiday with Mom. We joked about how it always seemed that winter would never end—

because on the East Coast you can distract yourself with the weather for hours or even days. We stared out at the landscape covered in snow like ash—a flat, gray deadness. We were both dreading the visit, but to talk about that was to give it some undue importance and to let it grow into words that could take shape in our anxieties.

Now that we were older, the visits were much more tolerable anyway. We had more control over these interactions. We arranged to arrive and leave on the same day, staying only long enough for a meal and never spending a night on some awful pullout couch. We would go. It would be terrible. We would leave unscathed. "Keep it quick and light" was my mantra.

When we went to see our dad on Christmas days, those Christmas Eves that we'd spent with friends and their families were always fresh in our minds: the smells of pine, cinnamon, cookies, and meals still settled into our pores; the warmth of families gathered around fireplaces; the conversations and silly games; staying up late and feeling welcome—like scenes from children's books. As much as any interaction with my dad was about what happened, it was also about what didn't happen. At Christmas, after being with families who cared so much about one another, his lack of consideration was obvious.

When we arrived to our dad's house, it was decorated and glorious—the perfect backdrop for a picture of a perfect family celebrating a holiday. There was a tree adorned with lights and ornaments, stockings hung on a brick fireplace, plastic ivy crawling along the windowsills, a manger scene set up on a coffee table featuring Jesus and his loving parents—even the sheep looking at him with adoration. It had all the same smells of our friends' houses—cider and cookies and roast chicken—but it was not the same. There was a particular crispness in the air, a chill. We exchanged hugs and kisses that happened without embrace and entered into the formality of discussions that sometimes reminded me of scripts for people learning a language: "Hello," "Hello," "How are you?" "I am fine. How are you?" "Do you like school?" "I like school very much."

We sat together: our dad, stepmother, and half siblings. Tom was a teenager then, and Annie a near teenager. Their family—the family who lived together in that house—had already celebrated Christmas. Lisa and I were the postscript to their holiday. "Merry Christmas," we exchanged in dull monotones. We were all watching the clock and wishing the afternoon to be over.

Anthony and I have raised our children Christian, which is another story, and Christmas in our house when the kids were young was a monthlong event of visiting Santa at the mall, making cookies, buying and wrapping gifts, decorating the house, and Anthony and I scrambling to fulfill wish lists. So much time and energy is invested in the buildup to Christmas day—when the kids end up playing with empty cardboard boxes rather than the expensive action figures the boxes once held. Then there is the cleanup of dead pine needles and packing ornaments back into boxes. I don't think that Anthony and I ever once thought it wasn't worth all of the work, time, and running around from one store to another looking for the correct version of some game. It isn't about Christmas morning, when the kids open gifts with the particular delight of having an expectation fulfilled, but the many small acts that precede that event and make our intentions—mine and Anthony's as the parents—so apparent to our children: We want to give our kids the world and especially give them the stability that Lisa and I craved as children.

Mom did that for Lisa and me during Hanukkah. Before the holiday she worked extra jobs so that she could fund her Hanukkah account. She collected our wish lists dutifully. She decorated the house and immersed us in the otherworldliness of ceremony. She lavished Lisa and me with gifts. We didn't go without. If everybody was wearing Guess jeans and that's what we wanted, we got Guess jeans. If the hot pink shirt with a collar was popular, she would buy us the hot pink shirt with a collar. She had a way of finding out what we wanted and needed and making sure that it appeared.

But at Christmas at our dad's house, Lisa and I were an afterthought. When we arrived that year to celebrate, Tom and Annie had already opened their gifts. They each sat in a pile of unwrapped, shiny, new, expensive gifts. Tom got an electric guitar and amp set, CDs, the latest tennis shoes. Annie had a new wardrobe, a bike, a boom box. It was like a department store had exploded all around them, the wrapping paper shredded down to confetti, the new boxes discarded in heaps, their gifts assembled and still bearing tags.

Most years this happened differently. Usually our dad and Janet had waited for us to arrive before the family opened presents. Then all of the presents had been crowded together under the tree. We weren't able to see how many were allotted to each person then, and in the shuffle of unwrapping, the count was always lost. But now we could see that only a few small things were left still wrapped under the tree, like the scraps left over on a table after the dinner had been eaten. It was difficult when injustices were laid so bare, a slap in the face that could not be ignored or denied.

I remember getting a snow globe, one that I still have. I collected them, and so it wasn't that it was a terrible gift, but that it suffered by comparison with the gifts given to my half siblings. I don't remember, but can imagine, the look on Lisa's face when she unwrapped her gift. It was the ugliest sweater you can imagine, one, she said later, meant for a blind old woman who never went out. It was beyond belief. These were white elephant prizes, discarded items our dad and Janet had found in discount bins. Last minute bargains. Lisa and I knew that no matter how we felt, we were supposed to act pleased and gracious when receiving gifts—Mom had taught us that—but it was difficult to pretend gratitude.

Headed home after the visit, Lisa and I burst out laughing. It was as though we'd both been holding our breath—and our tongues—since opening our presents. "Can you believe that?" "Can you believe what they got us?" "That was ridiculous." We laughed all the way home.

When we got home, we told Mom and laughed more. There was nothing to do but laugh.

Then Lisa said seriously, "I never want to go back there," and we all fell silent.

I agreed. It was, at the least, a disappointing waste of time.

Mom bit her lip in a way that kept her both from speaking and crying.

"Never. Never. Never," Lisa chanted.

* * *

Years later, very briefly, I revisited the issue of religion and holidays and their place in my life. Anthony and I had been dating seriously for a number of years, after dating on and off through some of high school and college, and were talking about getting married. Although he was Catholic, I had this strange and sudden feeling that if I had kids, they should be raised Jewish. I'm still not sure exactly where the notion came from. Religion really was not significant to me. I was not loyal because as a kid I had done everything: Christmas and Hanukkah, Easter and Passover. Religion was mostly about rituals and holidays and little about belief and spirituality. Likely my sudden opinion was a result of having cold feet about getting married; I grabbed onto the conflict of religion as an excuse to delay.

Before Anthony and I got married, and then again when I was pregnant with our first son, we agreed that we would not assign our kids any religion. We would allow them to explore everything. It seemed like a happy middle ground. But when Joe was born, and that absence became a reality, I thought more deeply about my relationships to the two religions in which I'd been brought up. There is an aspect of religion that is about identity. It doesn't even need to be as deep as a belief system. For me it may have been as simple as saying, "I am Jewish" or "I am Catholic" and really meaning it, and further meaning that I was a part of some larger community that claimed this as well. I believe that people can be more than one thing, including more than one religion, and genuinely so, but I somehow managed to feel a part of neither religion when I was growing up. I felt alienated. I had felt alienated all the years of my childhood without identifying the feeling. What I had first understood as guilt for my lack of loyalty to Judaism, and a sense of needing to side with Mom's honest history over my dad's fabricated past, I later understood to be a sort of mourning for a lack of belonging when I was a child.

What I had first understood as guilt for my lack of loyalty to Judaism, and a sense of needing to side with Mom's honest history over my dad's fabricated past, I later understood to be a sort of mourning for a lack of belonging when I was a child.

When Joe was ten months old, Anthony and I had him baptized into the Catholic faith. I realized that I wanted my kids to feel tied to something indefinitely. I wanted them to belong. They have all been baptized and been through sacraments, and we celebrate all of the Catholic holidays at our house. But we also celebrate the Jewish holidays with Mom and my extended family. Although my kids are officially not Jewish, they feel, in a very authentic way, that they belong to both traditions: Catholicism and Judaism. Somehow, by committing to one thing in favor of the other, they were able to embrace both.

The holidays are a strange time. They do not create crises in families but rather bring existing crises to the forefront. Those visible acts of decorating, baking, giving, and receiving gifts, and the ways people come together—or do not—display everyone's true characters and feelings toward one another. That may be why holidays are emotionally difficult for so many people. It isn't that they present new problems or triumphs but rather make the existing situation so apparent that it cannot be denied.

CHAPTER EIGHT
Deviant Behavior

Lisa

Lisa's favorite sport is soccer. She belonged to the 72-73 All-Star soccer team. Lisa also likes football and baseball. Her favorite rock group is Mötley Crüe. She was also on the student council in fifth grade. Lisa has an older sister, Sharon, in ninth grade. She also has a cat, dog, and rabbit. Lisa was in the fashion show in sixth grade.
—The inscription beneath my sixth grade yearbook photo

In my sixth grade yearbook picture, I am smiling. It is not one of those phony smiles that you strike for the camera: teeth clenched, muscles forcing your lips into a crescent. It is a real smile, almost a laugh. I am gleeful. I was twelve. I felt great despair when I was young, but in that smile there was still hope, as though for a moment—in a pause between the anxiety-riddled weekend trips to my dad's and the addictions that were about to take hold—I had come up for a breath of air. I still felt like myself. I was happy.

But my diabetes had an unfortunate side effect: The diagnoses declared that I was a sick child. My blood sugar levels continued to dip so low that it necessitated trips to the emergency room throughout my adolescence, reminding everyone who cared about me that my health was in jeopardy. Because Mom, my family, my friends, and my teachers were always worried about my physical health, they did not have time to be concerned about the other aspects of my life. They excused my misbehavior and blamed my poor performance in school on my health issues. No one challenged me academically. No one expected me to do better. No one called me out when I broke rules or obviously made no effort to succeed. It was a particular kind of sympathetic neglect. I did not believe that I could motivate myself. Instead I sunk to meet everyone's expectations.

I know that Mom and my family loved me completely and meant to nurture every part of my being; they never wanted to make me feel like they didn't care. Mom was working and raising two children on her own. She was giving Sharon and me every moment that she had. She didn't understand that those small, gracious acts of dismissing my misbehavior felt like she was dismissing me. She had no idea that I was dying inside. And I was incredibly good at hiding it. I didn't want her to worry about me or to feel bad for me. I never wanted anyone to feel as miserable as I felt, and so I gritted my teeth and smiled, I acted like things didn't bother me, I laughed with my friends, and I pretended to be fine.

During my adolescence and early adulthood, those pervasive childhood feelings of worthlessness and being unwanted festered, and I discovered new ways of dealing with them: drugs, alcohol, and an eating disorder. My teenage and young adult life would be shaped by my search for things to ease my pain or make me numb to my self-loathing.

I was fortunate to meet two good friends whom I knew throughout that time. I met one of my best friends, Christa, in seventh grade when we were twelve. The next year, at thirteen, I met and started dating my first boyfriend, Dillon, to whom, much like I had with Christa, I became incredibly close. Dillon probably understood me better than anybody I knew back then. His family life mirrored mine in many ways. He lived with his mom and sister and had a stepmother with whom he had a difficult relationship. Dillon was in my life for the next decade and a half. Christa and I are still friends today.

As young people, we hung out, talked, and acted as a solid source of support beyond what our families had to offer. We also started drinking. For Dillon and Christa, getting drunk was merely fun, but for me it was an escape from the entrenched sorrow I felt. I chased that escape as I grew older, at first longing for it, then needing it, then desperate to find it.

* * *

My understanding that I was not worth people's efforts was validated in high school. It became a self-fulfilling prophesy: My belief that my performance didn't matter justifying my lack of effort. The As and Bs I'd gotten in middle school became Cs and Ds by my junior and senior years of high school. My academic failure perpetuated the developing image that I had of myself as a fat, stupid girl. I was on a downward trajectory. I went from pretending not to care to truly not caring. I drank almost every weekend with Christa and gave up on being smart.

My teachers passed me as a way of getting rid of me. My sophomore biology teacher reported to my mother that I had earned a failing grade but he was giving me a D in order to get me out of his course. "Why should I make her repeat the class?" he asked my mom, "She just doesn't care; it won't do anything."

I was devastated when Mom told me what he had said. A heavy tightness sickened my stomach and brought acid to the back of my throat. I felt small, and dark, and empty. More than it humiliated me, it hurt to think Mom had to hear such accusations from my teachers.

Beneath the hurt I felt angry and frustrated with the world. My teacher had put into words the way I suspected the world perceived me. He had made it official. Whatever satisfaction I got from knowing that my suspicion was correct was quickly overcome by the sting of realizing what that truth meant: I wasn't worth anyone's time; no one cared enough to push me or to hold me accountable for anything. I was untethered, and there was no hope that anyone would rein me in. It was an awful, drowning feeling. I felt as though I were being swallowed from the inside. I was lost.

* * *

In brief moments things happened that proved that I had the potential to be so much more. Because my high school grades were poor, I didn't apply to universities. Instead, I went to Bergen Community College, which was ten minutes from Glen Rock. Although that year I lived at home with Mom, my life was completely different than it had been while I was in high school.

Most of my friends, including Christa, went away to college. I made new friends. But mostly I studied. I studied like I never had before. I was taking courses in things that interested me, like sociology and psychology. That year I got a 4.0 for the first time in my life. I was smart. I was a good student. My teachers liked me. I look back on that year and see all of the potential that I had.

But momentary success and redirection was not nearly enough to heal my wounded self. Near the end of my year at Bergen, I became bulimic. It was something that started slowly as a means of gaining and keeping control of my emotions and rapidly escalated, so that during the following year, when I transferred to Shippensburg University in Pennsylvania, the exuberance with which my addictive personality was able to terrorize my life became obvious.

With bulimia I lost weight, and that made me feel good. But more so, it felt correct to be seized by impulsive and compulsive behavior, to be overcome by cravings and urges, to witness my own behavior under the control of something that felt other than me and yet became me. None of that felt good. It was like there was an electrical current shocking me constantly, prickling across my skin with sharp jabs that penetrated my pores, piercing and loud and causing a pain that could be alleviated for brief intervals only by continuing the behavior.

It was like there was an electrical current shocking me constantly, prickling across my skin with sharp jabs that penetrated my pores, piercing and loud and causing a pain that could be alleviated for brief intervals only by continuing the behavior.

It got so bad that it could not be hidden. Mom was dating Bruce then, the wonderful man whom she would marry the next year. They were living together in her house in Glen Rock. When I went home during school breaks, both my weight loss and my strange eating habits were obvious. I remember Bruce once commenting to me, "Oh my God, you lost so much weight," and Mom hushing him with, "Bruce! She's not doing it the right way."

Then, during winter break, Christa caught me throwing up. I was humiliated.

* * *

I knew that something was wrong with me, but I didn't know what to do about it. That year was the first that I employed a tactic to try to heal myself that I would try again and again over the next decade: I made a change in geography as a way to change my life. In a new place, I could be someone new. Also, by the end of my first year at Shippensburg, too many people knew about me: my bulimia, my lying to cover the disease, and my occasional stealing—which started as sneaking food from other people. I was embarrassed and getting the wrong kind of attention. I was accepted to Rutgers—the school that Christa attended. It started a cycle of exhausting locations and the people in them, then leaving both as escape from the things I had done and the anger I had garnered and in search of a situation where I could be a better version of myself. It worked in small ways or for short increments, but eventually I always sabotaged myself.

At Rutgers I did make a change: I traded bulimia for a cocaine addiction. I had first tried cocaine at a party the summer after my senior year in high school. It was like I had found God. It was the greatest feeling I'd ever had. I had arrived. I felt seen. Important. It took away the negativity that fogged my thoughts, the insecurities that plagued my interactions. I felt like myself. I felt free. Cocaine was the whole that I had been searching for. Then, for years I had no access to it until I joined Christa's sorority at Rutgers.

This is awful to say, but I'm actually grateful to cocaine for saving me from bulimia. Bulimia intensified the hate I had for myself, diminishing me daily in devastating ways. In cocaine I found something that offered release from the voices in my head telling me what a bad person I was.

But cocaine was what ultimately broke me. I was entirely hooked. I would do anything for the relief—although temporary—from those feelings of worthlessness that had plagued me since childhood.

Cocaine also allowed me to continue the façade that I was coping, happy, and doing well. While on cocaine I could pretend normality. It wasn't like being drunk. I don't think my family ever knew that I was high during those years. There was never a risk that I would show up out of my mind, screaming, turning tables over, and ultimately ruining an evening. The risks were not public; they were personal, less dramatic, more covert, and damaging over time rather than in an instant. During the next years, cocaine shredded my life quietly.

Addiction presents as behaviors but is really a mental illness. For me that manifested not as raging drug-induced episodes but rather as exchanges and interactions that left my family asking, "What is she even talking about? What did she steal from me? What lies did she make up? What story is she trying to tell us now?" I was always sneaking around and covering for something. The secrecy distanced me from the people whom I cared about and also from my true self.

That summer I returned home to Glen Rock, where Mom was marrying Bruce. Life felt like it was beginning for everyone else and ending for me. Sharon was doing well. She had graduated with her BS in education and had a full-time teaching job in Paterson. She had been dating Anthony for what seemed like forever (although they took a short break that summer). Mom had found Bruce—or Bruce had found her. She was happy and starting what seemed a second life that would be full of love and joy. Dillon was planning to move across the country to go to university in Colorado. Meanwhile, I was floundering. I couldn't imagine what my life would be like with Dillon so far away. My world felt like it was collapsing.

My life as an addict hit several crisis points. One of those early moments occurred after I returned to Rutgers that fall. There I lived in a house with ten of my sorority sisters, including Christa, who comprised a makeshift family. I went to classes, or at least was registered for them. I attempted to go through the motions of being a student, but I was out of control. The lying that I was doing to cover my cocaine use, and my class absence, and disregard for others compounded with other smaller lies I told to try to feel better about myself or look better to everyone else. I couldn't keep track of my many deceits. I couldn't maintain the pretense of the life I'd fabricated there.

Mom could tell something was wrong from the strange phone calls she received from me. "Come home, Lisa," she said.

It was time, anyway, for another change in geography, a fresh start with people who didn't know me.

My departure was abrupt. I packed my things into my car without telling anyone where I was going. Christa tried to talk to me. "What's wrong? Where are you going?" she pleaded. I didn't know what to say to her. I just had to get out of there. I got into my car.

I remember watching Christa, tears flowing down her face, running desperately into the house as though she were going to solicit help. The look on her face was absolute devastation, this deep disappointment and fear. I was breaking her heart. It broke me. It seemed to only prove that I was as terrible as I believed myself to be. I felt awful, but I couldn't bring myself to face her.

Her expression and that image of her running away stayed in my mind all the way home and during the following months when I lived first with Mom, then with my dad. It was a feeling that I knew well. It seemed right that she was running away from me. I related to that sense of urgency, the panic, the need to get to one thing and away from another. Running seemed like the only answer.

CHAPTER NINE
Paterson

Sharon

I can be changed by what happens to me.
But I refuse to be reduced by it.
—Maya Angelou

After returning home from Ohio State University, I went to Rutgers to complete my degree. When I applied to the education program later, Rutgers informed me that they wouldn't take my transfer credits. I was looking at an extra year and a half of college. I transferred again to William Paterson University, just ten minutes from Glen Rock, and moved back into Mom's basement apartment. Lisa was a senior in high school. After she graduated and moved out, it was just Mom and me.

Mom and I were both very busy. We both worked all the time. I had several jobs in addition to my coursework: I was a nanny for a nearby family who loved me and worked at a store that personalized T-shirts, stuffed animals, toys, and candy for parties. On weekends I would visit Anthony, who was at Bryant University in Rhode Island, or visit other friends of mine who were nearby. A lot of my friends had returned home by then also, either finished with college or attending some place local, like me. We would go out in the evenings sometimes. I was always out, it seemed. Then coursework shifted into practicum experiences.

I finished college in five years. Three of them I spent at home. When I graduated, I moved to Hoboken.

The last year of my bachelor's program in education I had two student teaching assignments. One at a kindergarten through eighth grade school in the inner-city of Paterson, the other at an elementary school in the upper-class town of Ridgewood, where my dad lived.

In a perfect world, I would have started my teaching career in a town like Ridgewood. It was quiet, and easy, and familiar. I didn't want to teach in the inner-city, where my job seemed like it would be focused as much on social work as education. But after applying to several jobs the year after I graduated, the only interviews I was offered were for inner-city school systems. The school in Paterson where I'd completed part of my student teaching offered me a job as a teaching assistant. So I ended up back in Paterson.

I was terrified that first year. I was really out of my element. I had fulfilled my student teaching in Ridgewood in the kindergarten, which was the grade I was interested in teaching, but I was hired to teach seventh grade. I was twenty-three, from the upper middle class, mainly white suburb of Glen Rock, with a focus on and experience in teaching young children who arrived with brightly colored backpacks, shirts with cartoon animals embroidered on the chests, and excitement about lessons on counting and colors.

The seventh graders at Paterson ranged in age from twelve to sixteen and were mostly inner-city kids.

It was maybe because I sensed that I would not ever entirely fit in that I was reluctant to work at Paterson; but once I got there, I loved it. I was there for three years. Later I found out that the school had confused me with another applicant—a new teacher with middle school experience. She ended up teaching the kindergarten reading program, while I dealt with the preteens. I always wonder how my life would have been different if that error in paperwork had not occurred. Maybe I would still be teaching in the kindergarten in Paterson.

The school in Paterson was an old, outdated building, one of those formidable brick structures colored by mold and built on all sides to press against the street. There was a small dirt lot that the kids used as a playground. It had a single slide and a set of swings that hung from rusting chains. At recess the kids flooded into the black-topped parking lot, left vacant for their use. Around the school was a dilapidated neighborhood—where many the students lived—with rows of crumbling houses and storefronts with boarded up windows.

My classroom had scraped wooden floors and old desks. I spent the morning beating cockroaches out of the coat closet. There were no bulletin boards on which to post student work or learning materials. I ended up creating a makeshift display board out of paper duct-taped to the wall with a border of construction paper that resembled the tidy bulletin boards I was used to.

My seventh graders were mostly fragile kids who were acting tough. They had seen too much and dealt with situations beyond their years. They came to class hungry and afraid, exhausted after having been kept up all night by fighting parents or neighbors, having seen or experienced violence, drugs, gangs, prostitution, and the trials of guardians who were hanging on by threads or who had just let go. I was often heartbroken by the stories that appeared in the essays they wrote or that they scribbled on the desks when I wasn't looking. And I was also terrified by their behavior, which was often unpredictable, antagonistic, and on the edge of deteriorating into something worse. I often felt that teaching at Paterson was like being in a hostage situation—not as though I had been taken hostage by the students, but as though we had all been taken hostage together by some threat that came both from within and without. I was constantly negotiating, deescalating, and protecting. I always felt as though I were making decisions to save as many as possible, often at the cost of sacrificing planned lessons, defined rules, time, and the standards of education to which I was accustomed.

My situation at Paterson was complicated by the principal, a woman who was insecure, controlling, and generally worked to undermine and diminish the faculty. She frequently yelled at staff in the hallways as though they were children. I was told by an administrator to keep a written record of her behavior—which I still have in a journal—every rude remark and condescending lecture. She would call me into her office, sit me in a chair, put her face inches in front of mine, and yell about nonsensical things. She would tease me about the way I walked—"Slow it down, lazy," she'd yell in the hall, as well as "I guess nothing bothers you" and "You're too easy going. You need to get it together." She was horrible to many of the teachers who worked there, but she especially picked on me. I think that she hated that I came from the outside and was able to teach so effectively at Paterson. She was eventually fired.

Because of these factors, that first year was a major turning point in my life, or at least a time when I was aware in the moment of how much I had changed and grown. The old me would have quit; I would have walked out. I wanted to walk out a million times. I would drive down the parkway to school from Hoboken every day, and every day I would come to this fork in the road, one way leading to Paterson, the other way back to Glen Rock and my childhood home. Every day I would come to that literal crossroads and wonder, *Which way am I going to go?* "You're not going to quit," I would answer myself out loud. Almost every morning I would have to talk myself into going back to Paterson, but I powered through.

The three years that I was at Paterson, I taught a different grade level every year, so after my first year teaching seventh grade, I taught fourth grade the second year, and then third grade my third year. It was the principal's way of keeping me from ever feeling settled or like I had a solid foundation.

The last year that I was there, the school got a new principal and things improved. The school received funding for a state-of-the-art computer lab and adopted programs that benefited both students and teachers. I participated in a new educational program for faculty that evolved into a master's program—which is how I got my master's degree. In the program I reconnected with fellow educators in Glen Rock, including the man who had been my middle school principal. He actually remembered me from when I was a student. There was an opening at the school where he was working. "Why don't you come back?" he offered.

Until that moment I'd had no intention of leaving Paterson. I'd come to love the kids there, and I was really committed to them. But it was an offer that I couldn't turn down.

I felt guilty leaving the students at Paterson. They were mature in ways that were both sad and respectable. Long before the offer to return to Glen Rock was presented to me, my third graders would say, "Oh, you're going to leave us. You're not going to stay." Paterson was a launching place where teachers started their careers and left when they had enough experience to earn better opportunities. The turnover was phenomenal. The children felt the impact of that abandonment and the lack of consistency. They knew, better than me, not to trust any commitments I made to them.

But I couldn't deny that teaching at Glen Rock Central School was a good opportunity for me. When I started at Paterson, I wasn't married, I didn't have children, and I was able to dedicate myself entirely to my students. Three years later, my life had changed, or it was about to change. I knew that soon I would need time for my own family. And now, as of this book's publication, I've been at Glen Rock for twenty-two years.

* * *

Lisa was all over the place during the years I was finishing university and beginning to teach. She started at one school, came home, then transferred to Rutgers, where she joined Christa's sorority. The summer before Lisa started at Rutgers, when Mom and Bruce were married, I had just finished my first year of full-time teaching. I was living in Hoboken with friends and renting a beach house on the Jersey Shore that I went to almost every weekend.

One weekend I was there with some friends. We spent the afternoon drinking wine and margaritas and sitting out on the deck in lawn chairs improving our tan lines. I loved being there and being away from the chaos of my daily life. I felt relaxed. In the evening Lisa came to visit. We all changed into shorts and T-shirts but otherwise maintained our positions on the porch.

One of my friends went inside and did not come back out for a while. When she emerged, she looked panicked. She waved me toward her discreetly.

"The thing is," she whispered when we were sheltered together in the doorway, "I brought some cocaine."

I tried to nod. I hadn't known that she used.

"And it's missing," she told me.

I didn't know what to say—or, really, somehow I couldn't comprehend what she was asking.

"Someone took it," she clarified. "It was in my bag. Zipped up."

Whenever something went missing, I immediately thought Lisa was responsible, and that night was no different. Lisa couldn't be trusted. I knew that when we were kids, she had stolen candy from the trunk of Mom's car; when I was in middle and high school, she'd constantly taken clothes from my room; when I was in college, she had stolen things from the store where I worked. It wasn't that I suspected that Lisa had a cocaine problem, or even that I thought of her doing cocaine recreationally; I simply assumed that when something went missing, Lisa had taken it—for whatever reason.

I didn't confront Lisa then. My friend didn't want anyone to know that she'd had the drugs, so we didn't make a general announcement to the others: "There's missing cocaine." I was glad that she didn't want a production. I didn't want to deal with it, or with Lisa. The revelation that Lisa may have taken something from one of my friends didn't ruin my weekend, but it definitely put a damper on things.

I may have said something to Lisa about it weeks or months later, but I let the weekend pass without accusing her. I had to choose my battles. I often didn't confront her. I already knew the answers she would give and could imagine the lies that she would come up with.

Those conversations seemed pointless and predictable. "Did you do it?" I would ask. Lisa would offer some crazy story or get defensive and angry. I didn't want her to fly off the handle there at the beach house both because I did not want to deal with her and also because I did not want my friends to see us that way.

A few months into her second year at Rutgers, Lisa left college and moved home to live with Mom and Bruce. I knew that something was wrong because she disconnected from people with whom she had been close. It was especially shocking when she seemed to stop talking to Christa, her close friend of over a decade. Then, later, she moved out to Colorado on what seemed a whim. She was floundering, without any plans for her future.

By then Lisa and I had drifted apart. I had decided that she was a chronic liar. I never believed anything that she said. When she decided to leave the state, my first thought was not "Oh no, I wonder if Lisa is okay;" it was "Thank God she's going away." I was happy that she was leaving. It was stressful to have her close.

For Mom too it was difficult to have Lisa around. Mom was always worried about where Lisa was, and who she was with, and what she was doing.

I think also that as I grew up and had other things to worry about, I had less space in my life to worry about Lisa. Her problems seemed to pale in comparison to the problems of the students I was teaching in Paterson. Or maybe it was less that I compared these things and more that my new role as a teacher defined and limited my responsibilities: I was able to dismiss Lisa because I had other problems. I had things that I needed to do. I couldn't concern myself with her behaviors anymore. Solving problems at the school in Paterson was not only my job but also a more rewarding way of spending time. The other teachers appreciated me. And to the students, I was vital.

* * *

I remember having this exhale at that point in my life. I was so done with Lisa and dealing with all of her issues and behaviors. Somehow, at the same time in my life, I gained this incredible understanding and tolerance for people in circumstances that I had not previously considered. Teaching at Paterson introduced me to a kind of poverty and desperation that, during my years of growing up, had been only miles from my front door and yet had seemed to me like an entirely different, even fantastical world. These were difficult childhood situations far different than the difficult childhood situation to which Lisa and I had been subjected.

And while teaching at Paterson put things into perspective for me, it alienated me from Lisa. Rather than feeling more empathy for her, I felt less. Maybe it was because the bad behaviors exhibited by my students seemed justified by their backgrounds, whereas Lisa's behavior seemed to arise out of nothing. The challenges at Paterson were so tangible. They could be boiled down to the statistics of income, domestic disturbance calls to the police, and number of occupants per square foot. They were visible in the welts on a little girl's back, and the cockroaches crawling out of the coats hung in the closet, and the absence of lunches packed. Also I had a duty and specific ways of helping. I listened. I offered concrete advice. I reported abuse. I taught children to read and write in hopes that education would allow them to transcend their backgrounds. Lisa's behavior was amorphous and distant, by its very nature sneaky, allusive, and not conducive to labeling. At Paterson I felt like I made a difference. The students at Paterson changed for the better. They made small and large triumphs in learning and relationships. They reflected the care and respect I gave them. But Lisa seemed to be diminished by the trust I gave her. She took advantage. Her behavior became more devious. It was easy to hold her up to those students and dismiss her as hopeless.

If I had generally been more aggressive and direct about her behavior, rather than dismissive, maybe I would have come to understand her as an addict rather than a nuisance. But at the time, it was too much of a bother to accuse her.

I wonder what would have happened if I had confronted Lisa about the missing cocaine that summer in 1995 when she came to visit me at my beach house. If I had accused her of stealing, I may have revealed her drug problem. If I had generally been more aggressive and direct about her behavior, rather than dismissive, maybe I would have come to understand her as an addict rather than a nuisance. But at the time, it was too much of a bother to accuse her. I was not in a place in my life where I could truly acknowledge the problems that she was having.

CHAPTER TEN

Colorado

Lisa

The very unfunny cosmic joke: In an attempt to protect ourselves from pain, we perpetuate behaviors that create the very pain we're trying to avoid.
—Jen Sincero

We use expressions like "on the edge" and "falling off a cliff" to express the divide between safety and danger and those moments when people walk upon or cross the boundary between the two. This suggests that when you are safe you are on some kind of level, solid ground where you are in control. When you slip or fall or jump from that level ground, you fall into danger, pulled down by gravity in one swift move. But my descent was not a fall; it was a slow walk down a staircase. I did not slip from an edge and catapult downward in an instant; I slid down one step, caught myself and seemed to get my balance, then slid down the next step. The bottom seemed painfully far away.

I did not slip from an edge and catapult downward in an instant; I slid down one step, caught myself and seemed to get my balance, then slid down the next step. The bottom seemed painfully far away.

The summer after I moved home, Mom kicked me out. I had spent the remainder of the fall, winter, and spring sleeping through the day, rising only to go to work and make my daily runs to Paterson to buy drugs. I was dating another guy—I was always dating a guy. He did cocaine, as did most of the wait staff and the bartenders at my new job. I often stayed out all night, and Mom would drive the streets of Glen Rock and Ridgewood early in the morning looking for me. She'd ask me where I'd been, and I would tell her some obviously fabricated story. I was twenty-two and a total nightmare. She didn't know what to do with me. She told me to go and live with my dad.

I hated living with my dad, although, like so many of the emotions I associated with my dad, it seemed inexplicable. It was an imposing and present feeling, but one that I could not name or justify. I felt uncomfortable and unwanted but could not put my finger on exactly how or why in a way that would have made my feelings seem credible even to myself.

Then, at winter break, Dillon came to see me at my dad's house. Although we'd known each other since we were children, I had always purposefully kept my friends away from the house my dad shared with Janet. That winter was the first time I let Dillon see that space. I brought him over to the house when my dad and Janet were out. He walked from room to room before we descended into the basement where I slept.

Something stopped him in the hallway. He looked around. Then he looked at me, "Why aren't there any pictures of you here?" he asked.

They had pictures in the house of Tom and Annie, some with Janet or my dad or all four of them together. None of the pictures portrayed either Sharon or me at any stage of our lives. I had never noticed that Sharon and I were missing from the walls. We were not there: invisible, deniable, or not worthy of the tidy frames around Tom and Annie.

"How can you live in this house where you don't even have a room?" Dillon went on. "You live in the basement on a pullout couch. This is ridiculous."

At that point in my life, Dillon may have understood my relationship with my dad more clearly than I did. For years I had cried to him and told him that my dad hurt me, although I wasn't always able to understand or articulate exactly what transgressions my dad had inflicted. In that moment Dillon identified tangible proof that justified my feelings. "You can't stay here," Dillon said. "You can't live like this."

I thought he might be right. But I felt stuck.

* * *

I had a job at a bar down the street from my dad's house. The routine I'd had at Mom's continued to some degree at my dad's. I slept most of the day. Woke in the evening and went to work. Did blow after work with my new boyfriend and friends. Came home in the early hours of the morning to crash and started the process again the next day.

Living at my dad's house was awful. In the basement I stayed in a finished room on a pullout couch. The back wall was lined with storage closets, and off to one side was a laundry room. My dad was still a wine salesman then, and one of the perks of the job was free samples. In the laundry room, stacked in a wall of boxes and standing like bowling pins on the floor, were tons and tons of bottles of wine. I don't remember when it became part of my routine to drink the wine after returning home from work, but I think that it began very early. At 4:00 a.m., after stumbling home from a night of partying, I would make my way to the laundry room, sit on the pullout couch, drink wine from the bottle, and smoke a pack of cigarettes. I couldn't stop. And it seemed like I had little else in my life. After a few months, I was starting to scare myself.

One morning I came home from work, walked through the kitchen, and was stopped by a sight in the dining room: The table was cluttered with empty wine bottles. Janet, who snooped through everyone's things, had found them in my hiding place in one of the storage closets in the basement. The bottles were now in a crowd of transparent greens and purples that pushed all the way to the edges of the table—too many to count. Their labels were sticky and stained with drips of wine, their lips bore the jagged edges of plastic seals broken only enough to pop the corks out, and their arrangement on the table was haphazard and cramped. They were a ragged, beaten mob—an exhausted army and somehow a perfect physical representation of the past months.

Beyond the installation on the table stood my dad, Janet, and Sharon, waiting for me. I remember their stiff postures, as though they were bracing for something, and the looks from each: my dad with the averted eyes of a traitor, Janet glaring with disgust, and Sharon's look a complex of fearful, disappointed, fed up anger that seemed to say in some authoritative, near-motherly way, "Really? This is what's happening?"

"*What do you have to say?*" they asked.

I didn't say much. I didn't want to be there. I turned away and walked back door.

"You can't always run away," I heard Janet yell after me.

Those words have always stuck with me, or not so much the words but that they were coming from her—a woman who had abandoned six children, a master of running away.

Through all of my depression and addiction and years of being lost to myself, there were a few people who I was always honest with. Dillon was one of them. I had always been able to talk to Dillon; he was probably the closest person to me and understood me the best.

His words stuck with me: "You can't stay here." I knew he was right.

After the discovery of the wine bottles, I asked if I could return with him to Colorado.

"Absolutely," he said. He knew that I needed to get out of New Jersey.

When Dillon went back to Colorado a few weeks later, I went with him. It was January of 1997, and I was twenty-three. We packed our things into my car and drove. I left everyone and everything behind. At the time I felt no regret or remorse for all of the pain and worry that I had caused and was causing other people, especially my family. I wasn't thinking about them. I was thinking about escape. Immediately I was escaping my dad's house, but I was also hoping to escape something that I had been suffered for a much longer time. I needed to get away from the feelings that I had when I was at home. I needed to start over and clean myself up.

* * *

In Colorado I stopped using cocaine. I decided that I wanted to finish college.

After I'd been in Colorado for a year and a half, I enrolled in the University of Northern Colorado and took courses in sociology. I was especially interested in the study of deviant behavior and the mental illness of addiction. I made no conscious connection to my own life, but I was subconsciously searching for answers. I wrote several papers on topics that fit under one or both subjects.

Even before Colorado I had been interested in the study of mental illness. I was both trying to understand myself and also passionate about this research that was naturally easy for me to understand. It was foreshadowing of both my crisis and career to come. While I was a student at Shippensburg University, I had actually—somewhat accidentally—attended an AA meeting as part of a course. I had been assigned a paper about a twelve-step meeting, and I had happened to find an AA meeting. I went to a closed, members-only meeting.

I had intended to be a fly on the wall, an observer conducting research, but there were only eight people in attendance, and it was impossible not to be under the same spotlight as everyone else. People went around the table and told stories about addiction and recovery. One man with a few years of sobriety told a story of getting a ride home from work with a group of friends who started doing cocaine in the car. "I said 'No thanks' when they offered it to me," the man told the group at the AA meeting. Then he told his coworkers to stop the car and let him out.

Listening to his story, I thought, *How the hell did he get out of that car? How the hell did he decline the offer of cocaine?* In Colorado I didn't have access to cocaine, but I'm sure that if someone had offered it to me, I would have done it. To say no and to walk away seemed impossible.

I graduated at twenty-seven with a bachelor's degree in sociology and communications but still no real idea of what I wanted to do as a career. I hadn't used cocaine in nearly five years, but I was far from recovered, and even further from heading my life in the right direction. A shift in location and a transference of my obsessive behavior to academics had cleaned up some of my behavior, but inside I was emotionally dying and still walking that thin edge between normal-looking life and absolute disaster.

I remember one night, when I was out with Dillon and drinking, I broke down for no reason. I started crying in the car on the way home and couldn't stop. I can't even remember what we were talking about, or if we were talking at all. There were always tears right below the surface. The hurt of my childhood was always right there; the feelings of worthlessness and failure, that I was unwanted and never good enough chanted as a constant white noise in the back of my thoughts. I was crying so hard that Dillon pulled the car over and parked. I couldn't stop. I couldn't get myself under control.

It was the general accumulation of shame that had continued to thrive and grow within me. I couldn't name it.

"What's wrong? What's wrong?" Dillon was asking.

But there was no simple answer. It was the general accumulation of shame that had continued to thrive and grow within me. I couldn't name it. I just cried. It was one of the best cries that I'd ever had, but it did little to express the damage that had and would continue to destroy me.

I realized that I could escape cocaine by moving across the country but the sadness had stayed with me. Cocaine was a major problem in my life, but the larger problem was me, or it was in me. And I couldn't escape myself. No matter how much I tried to create distance, I was still there, somewhere deep inside.

CHAPTER ELEVEN

A New Life

Sharon

Just when the caterpillar thought the world was over, it became a butterfly.
—Chang Tzu

In 1997 Anthony and I got engaged; we were living together in Hoboken, and I had just started a new job at Central Elementary School.

The following year Anthony and I got married. We had a big, fancy wedding at the Newark Club in Newark, New Jersey. The ceremony was conducted by both a priest and a rabbi who alternated lines—the priest speaking in English and the rabbi speaking in Hebrew. We were standing under a chuppah that was decorated with lace and flowers. Anthony recited his vows in English, and I said mine in Hebrew. We did this largely for my grandparents—my mom's parents—who came from Finland for the wedding. They loved Anthony but were worried about me marrying outside of my religion.

After the ceremony, the reception was held upstairs in the twenty-second floor ballroom. It was an unbelievable space. The walls surrounding the room were floor to ceiling windows that looked out onto New York City. As the sun went down, the lights of the city came up under the purple sunset. It was breathtaking. We had a sit-down dinner and then a ten-piece band. The dance floor was packed all night, crowded with our friends, this sway of tuxedos and gowns, hands lifting up, laughter. I remember Lisa looking across the ballroom and saying to me, "Oh, that's just a mirror," but it wasn't mirror; it was a whole other room. At the time my father-in-law was the vice president of a major corporation, and a big group of his friends and coworkers were in attendance. It was a phenomenal night. I hear people say about their wedding, "I would never do that again. I would take the money and go on a trip or do something else." Not me. I would do it all again—in a heartbeat.

The one dark spot on our wedding was my dad, who did not attend. Nor did my stepmother, Janet, or my half siblings, Tom and Annie, who were young adults by then. I'd had some drama with my dad in the months before the wedding. When I told him I was engaged, he was genuinely happy. He offered to host the wedding but only on his terms: He wanted to have a small affair at an Italian restaurant that he liked in a nearby town. It wasn't what Anthony or I wanted. He was upset. He started picking fights with me about trivial things, some having to do with the wedding and some not. In hindsight, I think that he was only willing to attend a wedding on his home turf, where he had control over the situation. He didn't want to come to a wedding where the guest list would include his former in-laws, his own parents, and so many old (former) friends—people whom he didn't want to see. I don't think Janet could have tolerated such an event either. Instead of saying this, my dad picked at me, found reasons to disagree, and blamed me for things over which I had no control. Finally, I became frustrated and angry with him. I wrote him a letter and told him not to bother to come to my wedding.

Then our wedding announcement was published in the paper. It stated that "Marion and Bruce Kosman and Dorothy and Tony Bonanno are proud to announce the wedding of their daughter and son." My dad and Janet were not mentioned.

Janet was insulted. She called me to complain. Then she called Lisa in Colorado to say that she was hurt. Maybe she really had hoped to be included, but mostly I think that she was embarrassed by the public recognition of her and my dad's absence. The other embarrassment to my dad and Janet was that my dad would not be giving me away—a symbolic and visible act. I stopped talking to my dad and Janet.

The altercations with my dad and Janet were a bump in the road before the wedding. The wedding itself was perfect. Mom and my stepfather, Bruce, walked me down the aisle together. The only imperfection was that I asked Mom to dance the first dance of my wedding with me and she refused. She said that it would make her uncomfortable—she never liked to be the center of attention. I was upset with her rejection, and I know that she regrets the decision now. Instead, I played a song for her but danced with my grandfather.

My in-laws helped pay for half of the wedding, and Mom paid for the other half. I don't know where she found the money, but it was very representative of my family and my relationships with the members of my family. So many people were incredibly loving and supportive of me; my dad was not. In the end, I learned to enjoy life without him, but I always feel his absence.

* * *

A couple years later, Lisa finished school in Colorado and returned to New Jersey. It was about the time that my first son, Joseph, was born. It seemed like Lisa was constantly letting her guard down in issues related to her diabetes—not checking her blood sugar, losing track of her insulin, and getting low when she would come visit me or I would visit her. She thought of me as a caregiver. It was like she released the responsibility of taking care of herself every time she was with me; she knew that I would take care of her. I had to call an ambulance many times and kept orange juice in stock in preparation for Lisa letting her blood sugar get low while she was on my watch. Mom was immediately back in the worried state she'd occupied when we were children, always asking Lisa how she would manage various situations with her diabetes, asking if Lisa's blood sugar level was okay, and wondering how Lisa was feeling.

She thought of me as a caregiver. It was like she released the responsibility of taking care of herself every time she was with me; she knew that I would take care of her.

Lisa tells this story from that time that I don't really remember but I know still haunts her. When Joe was a year-or-so old, Lisa babysat him for a few days. Anthony and I had a daycare routine for Joe that had his care rotating between my mom, Anthony's mom, and a friend in the neighborhood who took him for a day or two each week. There was a week when Mom was out of town and I needed help with Joe. Lisa offered to stay with him. She worked nights at a bar in town and was busy with her own life, but she was free during the daytime, really loved Joe, and lived for spending time with him.

During my lunch break, I called Lisa from the phone in the school office to check in. Lisa didn't answer. I called back a few minutes later, then called again and again, letting the phone ring and ring. I was frantic. Glen Rock is such a small world; I remember that the secretary at that time was the mother of one of Lisa's best friends. I didn't need to explain much to her. She already knew that I had a young child and that Lisa was diabetic. We could both imagine the worst—fire, accident, something that had sent Lisa, Joe, or both to the emergency room. In the back of my mind, I knew that Lisa's irresponsibility was likely to blame. I considered the obvious even before I discovered it to be true: Lisa had put Joe down for a nap, then her blood sugar got low, and she passed out on the couch.

I asked the secretary to find a substitute for my class, left school, and went home.

Lisa was unconscious on the couch. It was difficult to wake her. Joe was in his crib, crying. I got Lisa some orange juice and helped to wake her up. I waited until she was fully conscious to yell at her. I was absolutely furious that I'd had to leave work and that she'd made me worry. My head was still buzzing with the anxieties of every terrible thing I had imagined. I really couldn't believe that Lisa had done that.

Lisa felt incredibly bad. She kept apologizing.

"When you were done yelling," Lisa reminded me as we were writing this book, "you asked if I could still babysit tomorrow."

She felt so bad about what she'd done that I likely knew she would never let her blood sugar get low again while she was watching Joe.

As we were writing this book, I realized how strange it is that I've forgotten some of these critical moments that Lisa remembers so well. That is how I've dealt with many issues related to Lisa—through a combination of checking out in the moment and selective memory retrospectively. It's probably one of the reasons that I have resisted therapy as much as I have—I have a sense that many things I've chosen not to acknowledge and remember could come out in those sessions, and I don't want to know them. I don't want those moments to be a part of my life. Therapy would have forced me to remember and, moreover, acknowledge—as has writing this book. When I say the words out loud, what I've spoken becomes my reality. For me it has always been a lot easier not to talk about issues and problems, especially if they are in the periphery and easy to ignore. If I don't talk about them, nobody knows about them, and I can pretend they aren't there. Writing this book has at times been painful or even frightening for me. Knowing that I completely forgot about Lisa passing out while she was babysitting Joe is just one example. I remember being panicked in the office at school when I couldn't get in touch with Lisa that day, but for me, before writing this book with Lisa, the story ended there.

* * *

It wasn't only Lisa's diabetes that was a problem then; she was becoming increasingly untrustworthy, and her dishonesty was starting to cause fights between Anthony and me. When it came to Lisa, I had blinders that Anthony did not. I knew that she lied, but I always believed there were limits to what she would do or say. Anthony saw things more clearly.

"Did you take that money I left on the table?" he would ask me.

"No. Why would I take it?" I'd say.

"I think Lisa took it." He'd make the accusation.

Things—mostly money—went missing after she'd been in the house. It was minimal amounts, pocket change and bills left over from small purchases. I would tell myself that Anthony had moved money that I'd set down but never ask him about it. Or I'd assume that I'd put it somewhere different than I remembered. I never wanted to consider the issue closely.

"How could you say that?" I said back to Anthony.

We got into horrible fights. I knew that there were things with Lisa that weren't right. I knew that she lied. But to accuse her of stealing seemed outrageous. His indictment was tangible and visible, hurtful both because he accused her and because the claim forced me to acknowledge the possibility.

Then we had a friend who mentioned to Anthony that he'd heard that Lisa was doing drugs. When Anthony reported this back to me, I quickly said, "He's just an asshole. He drinks so much. That's why he's saying things about Lisa."

Anthony decided not to engage in that fight, but it had planted a seed. In the back of my mind at the time, I wondered if there could be some truth to what Anthony's friend had said.

* * *

I was good at denying both the trouble that Lisa was causing and the trouble that she was in. I remember being at a party with Lisa once when we were younger, before she went to Colorado. I noticed all of her friends doing drugs, and I said to her, "How come all your friends do drugs but you don't?" I couldn't let myself even imagine that Lisa was also doing drugs—more than the occasional and recreational exception.

While Lisa floundered and struggled, my acknowledgment of her behavior existed on a spectrum ranging from flat-out denial to willful ignorance. It was rooted in the relationship that I'd developed over decades with my younger sister, starting with the afternoons when we were children and I pretended not to see her sneaking candy from the trunk of Mom's car; choosing when we were young adults to accept excuses for the things she did and did not do as related to her diabetes—and therefore not her fault; and as an adult finally denying that she was stealing money from my house. I lived in a kind of double mindset when it came to Lisa, subconsciously curating what I chose to know about the problems she was having and also selecting which of those problems to admit.

Avoiding accusation, claims, or even believing anything terrible about Lisa was also a family trend. Mom would not hear anything bad said about Lisa. If I would bring things to Mom's attention, she would have a million reasons for why those things were actually happening and were obviously not Lisa's fault. I think she knew that Lisa lied. I think that we both even understood that Lisa was not doing well generally, but it was easy to think that Lisa was struggling with deciding what she wanted to do with her life as part of a natural course of growing up, having problems with specific relationships, or being burdened by her diabetes.

In hindsight, there were many signs that Lisa was suffering. Lisa would seem odd or unhappy. Something about the way she related to me or spoke of how she related to other people or situations just seemed wrong. She would make decisions that I didn't understand. Suspicious incidents would occur in her presence. But nothing was obvious. There was nothing that I could put my finger on, no concrete evidence. I never saw her do drugs. I never looked at her and thought that she was high. I never saw her steal anything. It was easy to disregard those signals of her struggle that were abstract. I knew she lied. I knew she didn't control her blood sugar. But I didn't pause to reflect on why or search for some deeper cause.

It was later, when I had my own family, that I decided to eliminate nonsense of all kinds from my life, not only with Lisa but with my dad as well. There were other people involved now: Anthony, Joe, then Daniella and James. My priorities and expectations had shifted.

It was Lisa's lying that finally forced me to see the truth in all of the things that she did. I began to catch her in inconsequential lies—she would say that she'd been out with one friend when really she had been with another. I began to believe that she was lying about everything. Eventually, I couldn't listen to her at all. It was a terrible feeling.

There finally came that day when I absolutely knew that my money had been stolen and that Lisa was responsible. Lisa came for a visit, and when I went down to the basement to change the laundry, I heard her leave. When I went upstairs to see if she'd really left, I noticed money I'd left out on the counter was gone. It was a frivolous amount, twelve dollars or so, but I was certain that it had been there and that Lisa had taken it. I'm not a person brought easily to anger, but once angry, my response is volatile. With Lisa, that anger was what eventually fueled the intervention that got her help.

The first years of my marriage to Anthony were also busy with building my own family and career. My daughter, Daniella, was born when Joe was two, and my second son, James, was born a year and a half later—all three of my kids born before I was thirty-four. During those years I taught fifth grade. The day-to-day routine of feeding, dressing, driving kids to daycare, keeping up with laundry, reading books at bedtimes, dealing with the occasional midnight fever, coupled with planning lessons, grading papers, and working, filled my life and time.

The year I was pregnant with James, I switched grades from fifth to kindergarten. That year of teaching was especially difficult: I had two kids under the age of three at home, I was trying to remember how to teach kindergarten, and I would come home completely shot. I often felt that during the day I was just going through the motions, doing my duties as teacher and mom without investing or giving anything much thought. I didn't have time or energy to give attention to anything but the basic routine.

I taught two sisters then whose family closely mirrored mine and Lisa's childhood family. The younger sister was diabetic, their parents were divorced, and the sisters were being raised by their single mother. I took a vested interest in them simply because I could identify with them so much. I became close to the family. A few years ago, I received a message from the older sister on Facebook. She had become a teacher for children with special needs. She wrote me a beautiful thank you, saying that I was the reason that she had become a teacher. It was nice to hear that she was doing well and that I had been a part of that. Unconsciously, I think I was probably being the kind of teacher to her and her sister that I wished I'd had when I was young.

After Lisa graduated from the University of Northern Colorado and returned to New Jersey, she wrote me letters. She was falling apart, but even then I didn't realize to what degree. The letters were horrifically sad. They often started with announcements like "If you're reading this, I'm no longer living … " She was lost. Later she told me that she prayed that she would die. The letters were ramblings of self-pity posing as explanation or apology. They were broken and incorrect somehow, in the same way that Lisa was then, as though nothing about them did what it was meant to do or became what it was meant to be.

Lisa's letters made me furious rather than sympathetic. She went on and on in rants of feeling sorry for herself. When she acknowledged that she had done inappropriate things, it was as remorse for hurting herself. She never recognized the ways that her behavior affected other people.

This was during the years when I was embarrassed that Lisa was my sister. I always felt uneasy when I bumped into people who knew her because I worried that Lisa had done something terrible to them. I must have realized then that she was an addict, but I didn't admit it to myself or let it take the form of words and labels. I never said, "Addict." I never said, "Drugs." I never accepted that she had lost control of her life or that she was in danger. I knew that she was in a bad place. I kept myself from consciously acknowledging the terrible truth, the way I'd kept myself from verifying that Lisa had taken the cocaine that had been stolen at the beach house or the way that I had accused Anthony's friend of being a liar when Anthony had told me the friend had heard Lisa did drugs. I had an instinctual and immediate knowledge of the truth, but I quickly buried those thoughts in refusals, denials, and excuses. It was easier to be angry about Lisa's devastated letters than to accept that she needed help.

I was frustrated with Lisa when she returned from Colorado directionless and incapable. But I regret choosing to ignore what—I definitely knew later and could have known then—was a call for help. I wonder what would have happened if I had run after Lisa that day when I'd come up from the laundry room and noticed my money was gone, accused her, and demanded to know what was going on in her life that had allowed her to do something like that. It was easier to doubt my instincts, to manifest justifications, to sit on the couch, fold the clean clothes, and let Lisa go. I didn't tell Anthony about the money because I knew that he would declare it evidence of his consistent charges—proof that would become an indictment and lead to a course of action. If I had intervened earlier, could I have prevented a lot of the pain and struggle that was coming to Lisa's life?

On the other hand, although I was avoiding addressing Lisa's behaviors for the wrong reasons, I also think that at that point Lisa was not ready to be called out. I probably could have talked to her, but as she had when I confronted her with my dad and Janet in their house when she had been drinking all of their wine, I think she may have just gotten angry and run away. In the end, somehow, the way that Mom and I together approached Lisa on that cold morning years later—Lisa curled up in bed like a child, Mom past the point of worry and pushed to anger, and me no longer in a state of denial and willing to demand answers—seems the only way we could have gotten through to her. We all had to be ready.

In the end, somehow, the way that Mom and I together approached Lisa on that cold morning years later—Lisa curled up in bed like a child, Mom past the point of worry and pushed to anger, and me no longer in a state of denial and willing to demand answers—seems the only way we could have gotten through to her. We all had to be ready.

Although I had no idea what was going to happen, I felt so certain the morning that Mom and I finally intervened that talking to Lisa was the right thing to do. Mom looked so definite and strong then. I had, for the first time, really seen Lisa—how tired and weak she was, how beaten down and broken, how like a lost and scared child she was.

In memory, I can pull myself away from the intense feelings I had in that room for a moment and see the three of us in that space. Mom and I entering the dark room, the shadows of clothes on the floor and blankets on the bed blending in with the form that, underneath it all, was Lisa's exhausted body.

The light came on, bright at first, then warm. There she was. For a moment she stayed asleep, and I saw her round face. Framed in the covers, it looked so much like her face when we were children, me staring across a bed at her, watching her sleep, wishing she would wake. Mom and I pushed into the room, seeming to take up more space than our bodies could actually occupy, growing, filling the emptiness around Lisa. We surrounded her in a formation meant both to capture and embrace. There was a breath drawn in unison in a moment of silence. Then Lisa opened her eyes.

CHAPTER TWELVE

Wake Up

Lisa

Do the best you can until you know better. Then when you know better, do better.
—Maya Angelou

There's an expression that people use in recovery: I was sick and tired of being sick and tired. That's how I felt. Not only did I feel terrible, but I was also exhausted by feeling terrible, by feeling like my insides were swelling against my skin and then shrinking away into tight knots against my spine; from not sleeping, and from sleeping too hard; from reaching to a tickle above my lip and smearing the blood running down my nose across my cheeks; from being afraid that I would be caught, or that I would not be caught, or that somehow I would not be able to connect with my dealer, or that when I did connect with my dealer, I would not have enough money to buy what I needed; from lying to everyone about where I'd been and why, and from trying to keep track of those lies; from feeling suspect and ridiculed; from waking up with my head in a gray cloud, my body feeling too heavy to lift, and my legs feeling too shaky to hold; from going through the motions that now made no sense, so that if I paused to think and took myself off of autopilot mode, I would freeze, having no idea what to do or where to go next; from the anxiety of always being on that edge between making it through the day and not; from being disgusted with myself; from pretending. I was sick of pretending. I had been pretending for so long that I could no longer remember who I was beneath the practiced gestures. In truth, I was terrified that I was no longer there. I was depressed. Devastated. Broken. I couldn't go on. When Mom and Sharon appeared in my room that winter morning like phantoms that had grown out of the walls and stood so stoic, I was ready. Partly awake, partly asleep, partly dead, I thought they looked like guardian angels, watching me sleep. It may have been a dream. Then instantly it was very real. When I broke down and started crying, it was the best thing that ever happened.

After I graduated from the University of Northern Colorado, I returned to Ridgewood and my old life. I went back to work at the bar where I had been a cocktail waitress, I found my old friends, and slipped back into my old routines—which fit like a second skin. I was doing cocaine every day again. I was twenty-seven.

* * *

When I moved back to Ridgewood, I bounced around between jobs. At one point I was working with a well-known liquor and wine distribution company in New York City to make selections about what products to keep in stock. I was good at it. I liked it. But my cocaine habit was getting expensive and interfering with my sales routine. I had to quit.

I finally found a job bartending at an establishment called Miller's that Anthony's family frequented. Bartending allowed for a schedule that I was more accustomed to, and it fueled my bad habits. I slept all day, worked at night, went out afterward, and returned home to crash in the early hours of the morning. That lifestyle was the nail in the coffin of any chance that I had to maintain a real life.

* * *

Despite the chaos that would come during my time working at Fratello's, I was lucky that the family who owned the bar was really good to me. They had two sons. One of then, Paolo, and I did cocaine covertly behind the bar while we worked. The other was Carlo. After close one night, Carlo and I were alone together straightening things behind the bar, and I turned to him and said, "I'm so fucked up. I can't stop doing cocaine. I don't know what's the matter with me." The words had just come out, maybe because I was too exhausted to hold them back, or maybe because of that look Carlo always gave me that was genuinely concerned without being judgmental.

He nodded, listening but not alarmed. We moved to the other side of the bar and sat for a minute on the stools usually occupied by customers who wanted as much to talk as to drink. He was speaking to me in this soft, gentle voice, as though coaxing me from the breakdown he could see opening like a hole in my future. He told me that he would help me. He also told me how hard it would be to quit.

"You're high again!" He accused me days later and many days after that.

Carlo's guardianship wasn't passable route to recovery when I was still getting wasted with his brother. Carlo just became yet another person I had to avoid or lie to on a daily basis. It was a typical example of the attempts I made to get help in those days.

* * *

My pain was cumulative, not only the physical pain from the damage I did to my body those years after I returned to Glen Rock but also the emotional pain collected like stones that I had carried since childhood. I carried them in my mouth, their jagged edges pressing against my soft gums. They slid down my throat and sat heavy in my chest, nearly blocking my airway. By the time I was thirty-two, I had beaten my body and mind into a ruined submission. For years I'd been doing cocaine every day. For even more years I'd been lying and stealing. For almost my entire life, I had felt lost and unworthy in some inexplicable way for which there seemed no cure.

For years I had been losing people like a tree in winter losing leaves. People dropped out of my life and blew away without a trace, a few here and there at first, then more and more, until there was nothing left but the cold. No one wanted to be around me.

I would spend my time driving out to my dealer's apartment building on the Upper West Side of Manhattan with my one real friend at the time, Matt—who is no longer alive—and do cocaine at the same kitchen table where our dealer would have meals with his wife and teenage daughter. As if in some perverse sitcom, Matt and I would sit down like dinner guests and do drugs while our dealer's family was a room away.

When I had found myself in an abusive relationship, I had pushed away nearly everyone else close to me, and Matt was the only person in my life I could turn to. With what capacity he had to help, he came to my rescue. I would have been on the streets at one point if it hadn't been for him. I knew that I was in trouble.

In the meantime I was disappearing. Fading. Evaporating into the air. Every day I lost more and more of myself. The drugs were no longer working to make me feel better, although I persisted in administering them in hopes that they would be effective. I was deeply sad. I cried every day, not the soft whimpering of a woman overburdened but the loud, uncontrollable, choking sobs of a child desperate and frightened. I wrote letters to Sharon and Mom. When I went to sleep, I prayed to God. "Maybe I don't need to wake up tomorrow." I was too cowardly to take my own life, but at the same time, I couldn't go on.

One night I called Mom crying and left a message.

The next day, when my nose was so clotted with blood that I could not breathe—something that happened routinely—I went to the hospital and sat in the parking lot, my car running. I was too weak to go in and lie to the receptionist. I called Sharon.

I was certain that I was only hurting myself. I was ruining my life, but it was mine to ruin. "I'm not bothering anyone," I often told people. I might have repeated that phrase that morning in my room when Mom and Sharon woke me first with the light, then with the bombardment of questions and claims for which I had no answer. How could my doing drugs be hurting them? They'd never even seen me do drugs.

"How could you do this to me?" Mom screamed. She was so angry that her face was red and her lower lip trembled. I had rarely seen Mom like this. I could not remember the last time she had yelled at me in this way. "How could you do this to Sharon?"

I had already sworn at her and Sharon had already yelled at me. The shock of hearing myself curse at Mom held me silent and frozen. I felt not only shame but also the awareness of the shame. My feeling took shape. I realized: I hate myself. I hate being like this.

Sharon took a breath and spoke calmly. "Can't you see how worried we are?"

The world that I had been living in the past years had been a kind of illusion, a nightmare that I had dreamed and lived as though it were real. It shattered then. What was left was the pale pink room, the house that smelled like fresh paint, the radiators clicking, and my sister and Mom sitting on the bed on either side of me, their arms bracing me, cradling me. I couldn't stop crying.

The world that I had been living in the past years had been a kind of illusion, a nightmare that I had dreamed and lived as though it were real. It shattered then.

It was unbelievably bright outside. Mom and Sharon walked on either side of me down the snow-dusted sidewalk toward Sharon's car. They each carried bags of my clothes. It was cold. They had wrapped my winter coat around me, but the crisp air bit gently at my bare cheeks. I remembered someone telling me once about letting fish nibble at their toes to clean away the dead skin, and bacteria, and dirt. A cleansing. The air felt clean. The sun lit the snow so that it was as though light was coming from all around us. Tears drying on my face froze in stiff streaks that seemed to hold my eyes open as I tried to squint. I put my hand up to shade my eyes, but the glare was too intense.

I moved home with Mom while I tried to find treatment. I was trying—and failing in spurts—to stay off of cocaine, but other than that my life remained the same. I was still bartending at Miller's. I was still hanging out with all the same people. Days passed, then weeks, then a month, then two.

One evening I got a call from someone whom I worked with at Miller's. He attended community college. After classes he'd gone out to his car and it wouldn't start. We were scheduled for the same shift that evening. "Can you come pick me up?" he asked.

"No problem," I said.

I didn't realize how low my blood sugar was.

I remember getting in my car, but the rest is a fog until I drove through the red light. I remember honking the horn. It was like I could process the moment just enough to know that something was really wrong. I was warning other drivers away without really knowing why. I coasted through the light, the horn blaring.

Then I heard the sirens. A police car pulled up alongside me. I drifted over and parked.

The officer pinned my car to the side of the road with his front bumper. He leaped out and banged on the window. When I opened the door, he was talking. I tried to respond, but I couldn't feel whether or not my lips were moving. It was like this fuzz that had started at the periphery of my vision, framing the world, was slowing closing in. I was already falling into the cloud that was overcoming me. The officer, the street, the car were visible only in the last clear point at the center. I kept falling. They kept getting smaller and smaller, further and further away.

The other two police cars seemed to manifest out of nowhere, so that one minute we were a quiet scene on the side of the road, and in the next instant we were the chaos of flashing lights. I was only slightly aware of the audience of other officers, gawkers out in the neighborhood, people peering as they drove past. The officers seated me on the curb as they continued to search my car and question me. They thought I was high.

It wasn't until I went into a diabetic seizure that the officers realized that I was in trouble. They rushed me to the nearest hospital.

When I woke up, I was handcuffed to a hospital bed, and the two officers who had brought me in were sitting in hard plastic chairs at my side. They stood and leaned over me as I opened my eyes. They were talking lightly to one another. "Is she up?" "She's up." "Call the nurse."

"Can you hear me?" one of the officers said.

"We wanted to wait and make sure you were okay," he told me after the nurse came to check my vitals. "We're really sorry, ma'am. We found drugs and assumed. We didn't know that you were in need of medical attention. You're in good hands. These people are taking good care of you. We're going to stay here with you until it's time to take you back."

I felt oddly safe, tethered to the bed by the handcuff on one side and to an IV drip on the other, with the doctors, nurses, and officers in their uniforms following procedures. They were helping me.

When I was released from the hospital, the officers brought me to the station and Mom picked me up.

My court date was a few days later. "I need help," I told the judge.

"Get yourself some help," the judge told me, "and we can expunge this."

It was the push that I needed to become serious about finding treatment. Although I stopped working after my arrest, my boss at Miller's let me stay on the company health insurance. He wanted me to get better.

It was the end of February. I found an ad in the Yellow Pages for a detox and treatment facility in New Jersey called West Oak Treatment. They didn't have any beds available, but they put me on a waiting list. The person who answered the phone at their call center told me to hang in there. "A bed will open up soon," he promised. Then he called me every day afterward to ask me how I was doing and to reassure me. "We are saving you a bed. It's your bed, and it will be here for you. You can do this," he would say.

A week after I first called West Oak Treatment, on March 7, 2006, a bed became open, and I officially entered recovery.

Years later, when I was working in recovery, I went back to West Oak Treatment and asked to go into the call room. It was filled with booths, each with a person holding a phone to his or her ear, lifelines to people on the other ends of those calls. I explained who I was in hopes that the man I had spoken with was still there, but no one remembered me. "All of you in here," I said to the operators, "you helped save my life."

My insurance would only allow me to stay at West Oak Treatment for a few days, but West Oak Treatment then sent me to a treatment program in Florida that my insurance would cover for months. Drug treatment in Florida at that time was amazing. They not only helped clients to recover physically, mentally, and emotionally but also taught us how to move forward as recovered, healthy people making new lives for ourselves. They taught practical life skills, took us to AA meetings, and showed us how to live outside of the recovery center.

Florida drug treatment not only saved my life, it became my life. I became a marketer for drug treatment in Florida, working for a company and making trips to other states to help people move from short-term detox centers into long-term treatment centers in Florida. I was good at it. Most people in my position could maybe get five or six clients a month to agree not only to go into treatment, but to move out of state to Florida to do so. I would get thirty to thirty-five people a month into the treatment center where I worked. It was unheard of. I was a natural. I really believed in treatment in Florida, I related to the clients, and I was willing to talk about my own experience. I genuinely cared. I had finally found my calling.

PART TWO

Better Together

I'm thankful for all of it. The highs. The lows. The blessings. The lessons. The setbacks. The comebacks. The love. The hate. Everything.
—Anonymous

CHAPTER THIRTEEN
Recovery

Lisa

We are all broken … that's how the light gets in.
—Ernest Hemingway

Recovery is a process. Think of it like an onion—there are layers and layers of growth and treatment that you must go through as you work on self-awareness and self-discovery. First you must rid your body of toxins and stabilize your physical person through detox. This requires hospitalization or admission to a medical facility. When you are a drug addict and you stop using drugs, your body goes into withdrawal; it revolts. Your system has adapted to functioning with a steady stream of poison, and now without that poison, your body is thrown out of balance. You feel sick. You sweat. You have excruciating headaches. You grow cold and then hot and then sweat and then shiver. Your body feels foreign. Often you don't know how you feel. You feel like you're going to die.

In detox, patients are monitored around the clock by nurses who check on them frequently, sometimes as often as every ten minutes. Many patients are medicated to help control symptoms. The body is tossed into a sudden peril that at times can be dangerous. Patients spend anywhere from seven days to one month in detox in order to completely rid their systems of drugs. I was in treatment for one week in New Jersey, and then I was sent to Florida for extended treatment.

Florida treatment, at that time, was different than treatment in all other parts of the country for a couple of reasons. One reason was that it taught patients how to live—something they had stopped doing while they were in active addiction. Later, when I started working in treatment, I taught my patients how to vacuum, wash dishes, do laundry, balance a checkbook, make a budget, shop, organize groceries in kitchen cupboards, make to-do lists, keep calendars, and all of the other mundane stuff that makes life livable. These are little, basic things that people learn through experience as they grow up—experiences that people don't have or learn from when they are using drugs. To be able to do these small things is to be able to manage your life day by day, to take control, to become independent, to be responsible. It feels good.

The other reason that Florida treatment was so superior to treatment in other states was that it enabled insurance to pay for longer stays. Whereas in New Jersey my insurance only covered five days of treatment, in Florida it covered months. It gave me, and more generally gave addicts, time to recover.

* * *

When I was nine months sober, I got a job in Florida working at a private detox center. At the time it seemed like an opportunity to reenter the world as a functioning, working person. It ended up being the first step in what would become my new life and career. I always wanted to be a therapist. I am a good listener. Since childhood I have related to and held onto other people's pain. When I first got sober, I realized that people—both those whom I knew well and those that I'd just met—felt comfortable talking to me about emotional and personal issues. People would tell me their life stories—every single problem they'd ever had. They would tell me about their childhoods, about sexual and physical abuse, about heartbreak. I may have trained formally in sociology, but the reason I was good at listening to them and understanding them was because I had been just like them; I was just like them. Therapy seemed a fitting career path for me. I wanted to help people.

The detox center was called West Haven House. It had the appearance of a large, cozy house. Two people shared nicely furnished bedrooms with their own bathrooms and televisions. There was a living room with overstuffed couches and a kitchen where a chef cooked meals for the patients. The back of the house opened onto a deck where patients could sit on lounge chairs under sun umbrellas and look out on a pond. It was a really nice detox center designed for patient comfort and well-being during their recoveries. I worked as an assistant, helping with administrative and organizational tasks—filing, answering emails, and completing paperwork behind the scenes.

West Haven House was owned and run by a family of siblings. What I learned then and during the next decade is that many people working in detox and recovery centers are in recovery themselves. This was true of the owners and many of the people working at West Haven House.

A boss with whom I would work much later used to say, "We work with very sick people. And then there are the clients." Recovery is something that people enact on various levels; it happens on a spectrum: Some people continue to work hard at it and live well, others do the bare minimum and struggle. Most of the people who were in recovery and also working in the recovery industry were not using drugs, but they were also not taking care of themselves or working daily on their recovery. This is referred to as being a dry drunk. When you don't work at recovery, all of the defects in your character come forward.

People emerge from recovery with all of the human flaws and emotional damage that brought them to drug addiction. In addition, they have learned behaviors as active addicts that still come very naturally: temper tantrums, lying, showing up late, forgetting appointments, not completing tasks, being casually and detrimentally inconsiderate of other people. Working on your recovery means working on these behavioral issues and the emotions at the root of your addiction. Dry drunks do not cull this behavior or face their emotional demons. Dry drunk behavior is ultimately self-destructive and, as I learned in the treatment industry, it can also destroy a community. Dry drunk behavior was so pervasive in the treatment industry when I worked there that it changed the culture of the business. Things that wouldn't have been acceptable in other industries—missing meetings, coming in late to work—were tolerated in the treatment and recovery industry. At West Haven House, I learned that it made the working environment difficult and made accomplishing anything challenging. The family members who owned West Haven House were mainly dry drunks or, in a few isolated cases, active addicts. The result was dysfunctional and often childish management of the detox center.

While at West Haven House, I started to work toward a Certified Addiction Professional (CAP) degree, which would allow me to be a counselor—something akin to being a therapist. Part of the degree required me to have a certain number of hours working with patients. The owner of West Haven House let me run support group meetings so that I could earn hours. Running a support group in detox is comical. The patients are medicated to help them withdraw safely. This makes them conscious but shell-shocked and dazed. I would sit with five or six people on comfortable chairs on the patio outside and talk, their focuses wandering as they rambled about what they loved or hated about detox, anxieties they had about the present or future, troubles that they were facing. We also talked about TV shows, music, hairstyles, food, and the unrelated issues that interrupted their thoughts with dire importance.

This was when people started to really talk to me in a way that they didn't talk to other people. I heard terrible and devastating stories of abuse, loss, and things people had done and could never take back.

At West Haven House, discharge planners also met with clients individually to try to convince them to enter treatment programs once they'd completed detox. The system has since changed dramatically. Now people are sent to detox centers by treatment centers, so that their release back to the treatment center after detox is automatic. But then, patients had to commit to treatment independently.

After I had been running support group meetings for a while, one of West Haven House's discharge planners went on leave for two weeks, and I was temporarily promoted to his position. I was very early in my own recovery then—less than a year in—and my own experiences were fresh and present. I really connected with the patients with whom I met. I talked to them about my own treatment. I told them that recovery had saved my life. All of the treatment centers in Florida were working in a model that was focused on preparing patients for long-term success with practical, real-life experiences. Not only were they taught life skills but also taken to outside AA and other support group meetings, where they found sponsors and started building a network of support beyond the treatment centers.

I surprised myself during those two weeks. I convinced everybody with whom I worked to go into treatment. I was a natural. I was selling the path that had saved my life, an idea that I truly believed in. People felt my sincerity and commitment to recovery programs. There was no bullshit. I had absolute faith in Florida treatment. In those brief two weeks, two administrators at local recovery centers took notice of all the patients I was sending them: Ed Esposito of Place of Healing and Jim Langston of Be Well Now.

* * *

I was getting to the end of my rope with the dysfunctional management at West Haven House. I wanted to leave, and I inquired about getting a job with Place of Healing, but Esposito wouldn't hire me. He said I was overeducated, and he was right. As disappointed as I was that I couldn't be a part of the great work Place of Healing was doing, I knew I could only have been hired on as an underpaid and overworked tech—the backbone and the busboys of the industry. I would have left that job in two seconds.

When I finally I couldn't take it at West Haven anymore, I quit without having another job lined up. I approached Jim Langston then. He saw that I was desperate and agreed to let me start in a position the following Monday.

I started at Be Well Now in the phone room with a plan to become a therapist. I now was the voice on the other end of the line, that voice that had calmed me down not long before and told me that I could make it, that a bed would become available and I would get help. I knew exactly how people calling into the center felt, I knew how to talk to them, and I knew how to listen. I could motivate them to make changes in their lives. I was very at home in that job. My focus was on getting people into treatment and thereby saving their lives—the way my life had been saved. Patient by patient, I talked people into treatment. I convinced tons of people to enter treatment, and the management took notice, especially the owner.

Eventually I came full circle. I was promoted into a marketing position and sent to live in New Jersey to promote our Florida treatment facility at New Jersey detox centers—New Jersey health insurance translated well to Florida treatment, and because of this, the Florida recovery market targeted patients in New Jersey.

I went to detox centers in New Jersey and presented alone to large groups of administrators, therapists, and discharge planners, explaining treatment in Florida and promoting Be Well Now. When I started I was excited and also deathly afraid. My first presentation was at a detox center called Recovery Clinic. I bombed. I wasn't expecting the bombardment of questions that followed my carefully constructed and practiced presentation. A lot of the questions were about insurance, which was one of the main selling points and something about which I didn't know enough to respond well. The interrogation revealed to my audience, and to me, how little I knew about the treatment business.

If that same presentation happened now, I would be able to fully answer all of the questions asked. But back then I was like a sheep sent to wolves. The people at Recovery Clinic were tough on me, and I left feeling inadequate and devastated.

When I got back to Florida, I went to Langston, and I told him, "We're not going to get any patients from Recovery Clinic. You've got to come back with me and talk to them about insurance."

Langston went back with me to Recovery Clinic two days later. At the start of our follow-up meeting, I explained, "I'm really sorry. I'm new." Honesty was my new status quo, and the people at Recovery Clinic appreciated both my sincerity and my initiative to make sure that all of their questions were answered correctly.

I was learning on the job, and I was learning fast. Recovery Clinic became one of my best referrals. None of the other treatment centers in Florida had been able to win their support. I was shocked that they believed in me. I had a realization: Maybe I'm really good at this. Up until then I'd thought that I was just lucky. I was still plagued by low self-esteem, but something about winning Recovery Clinic changed the way I viewed myself. It was proof that I had talent.

I took the New Jersey treatment industry by storm, winning the support of detox clinics and hospitals and taking business away from other Florida treatment facilities. I got West Oak Treatment, where I had first been admitted. I wasn't selling them something; I was telling them my truth. I believed in Florida treatment. They knew that I was genuine.

While working at Be Well Now, I got married for the first time. It was very early in my recovery. I was so dedicated to my job that I went to Florida to do an intervention the day before my wedding and flew back that night, ten hours before the ceremony. I had always been a hard worker but was exponentially more so while working in the treatment industry because for the first time in my life, I believed in what I was doing. I was inspired and committed to helping people.

* * *

Still, I made a lot of mistakes while in early recovery, in both my personal and professional life. I was not using drugs, but I had also not changed my behavior. I was still struggling with the hurt that had brought me to addiction in the first place. I treated many people who entered my life while I was in early recovery badly. They deserved so much better.

My first marriage was a major error in judgment. I was incapable of being in a relationship. As with many of the mistakes that I made then, I knew at the time that what I was doing was wrong—in early recovery you are told not to get involved in relationships—but I did it anyway.

> I was not using drugs, but I had also not changed my behavior. I was still struggling with the hurt that had brought me to addiction in the first place.

That may have been one of the most difficult things about my recovery. Although I was no longer using drugs, my struggle was not over. I still had work to do and issues to overcome. Inevitably, three and a half years into my sobriety, my first marriage ended in divorce. I didn't want to be with anybody after that. I was sick of hurting people.

I remember one night going home, looking in the mirror, and crying hysterically. I couldn't believe that I was still hurting people. "How can you still be doing this after so many years?" I asked myself. I was now thirty-six and still acting without considering how my behavior impacted other people. I needed to make a change. I needed to focus on getting to know and improve myself. I stopped dating for the next year.

When I was going through my divorce, I moved on from Be Well Now and got a new position at Place of Healing. By then Ed Esposito was no longer working there, and it was owned by a man named Bob Jones.

I learned a lot from Bob. He ran amazing groups that really helped people to connect to one another and discover things about themselves. He cared a great deal about the patients and loved his job. He had a mindset that carried over to the entire staff: We were working to give our clients better lives.

Still, he taught me that you can be passionate about what you do but must at the same time make economical decisions for your business because the recovery business is, in fact, a business. Most times, what was good for the business was also good for the clients. In the recovery business, you get used to the heartbreak of relapse. Clients return constantly. You have to know when to say, "No more." Recognizing when your investment is not working is a sound business practice, and, moreover, allowing people to reenter treatment as though it has a revolving door is enabling bad behavior and ultimately prevents clients from ever truly recovering.

As incredible as Bob was at his job, he was also a very dysfunctional human being who created dysfunction at work. Like many people whom I've met in the treatment business, Bob had recovered from his own addiction, but not from himself. He was a narcissist. He played mind games with the staff, turning us against one another and creating competition between people where there didn't need to be any. He eventually relapsed.

In many ways, Bob reminded me of my father. Bob could command a room, but he didn't have one close friend. He also had a daughter from his first marriage whom he disregarded, who also happened to be an active addict.

One day, Bob asked if I would talk with his daughter to see if I could help get her to stay in treatment. Bob was a therapist. He should have realized how close my own situation was to his daughter's—a young woman estranged from her father and in active addiction. I had no perspective and talking to her retraumatized me.

I was furious after speaking with her. "I wish my dad was still using," she told me, "because that at least would be an excuse for why he never wants to see me." I was like her. I was the forgotten daughter. I felt her anger like it was my own, and I was angry that Bob had been so insensitive to my personal situation when asking such a favor of me.

I stormed into his office and yelled at him, forgetting that he was my boss. I told him that he was a terrible person and a terrible father. We got into a huge fight, made personal because we had become close friends. He later apologized for putting me in such a position, but Bob was also my boss, and my confrontation was unprofessional. He sent me home.

* * *

This is what the universe does: It keeps giving you the same situation until you deal with it. Encountering Bob felt fated. I had to deal with the unresolved issues I had with my dad by dealing with Bob—a surrogate father. As difficult as working with Bob was and as trigging as the situation with his daughter was, the experience allowed me to reckon with my feelings for my father in a way I never really had before. Because of that, Place of Healing was a place of growth not only for the patients but for me as well—not just because of all of the learning opportunities I found in Bob, but also because it was where I met Chris, the man whom I would later marry. Chris had made the same mistake I had: He had gotten married in early recovery. Chris had married in his early twenties, when his first wife, Heather, had gotten pregnant. When I met Chris, he and Heather had two children who stayed with Chris every other

This is what the universe does: It keeps giving you the same situation until you deal with it.

weekend. He was also going through a divorce with his second wife at the same time that I was going through the divorce with my first husband. Both of our relationships had started in early recovery; both of our marriages had lasted less than a year. Chris and I became good friends. He asked me out nearly every day. It became a joke. He was the king of one-liners: “How’s my future ex-wife?”

Although I had decided to be single, Chris had a few things going for him. He was persistent, kind, and good looking. One day, after we had been friends for years, I said yes to his routine request that I go out with him. I don’t know what changed my mind. We went out for coffee, and then we went out for ice cream. Things started slow.

* * *

During this time, I also began working with Ryan, a man whom I’d met in our respective first years of recovery, and who also worked at Place of Healing. He was the reason I got the position of Place of Healing, and he would also later become my business partner. Ryan knew how to make money, and I knew how to keep people in treatment.

Ryan and I had also made connections and met some good people in the recovery business. Both Ryan and I brought former coworkers—including my new husband, Chris—on board to work for our new recovery center. We partnered with Alex Brown—someone whom Ryan had worked with previously—who gave us a business loan. We called our business Journey to Joy.

Those first months I worked intense hours. I was engaged in a process of learning by trial and error. I came from the intervention side with the ability to empathize and assist clients but did’t understand the business side until I was in the middle of it. One day Brown and Ryan came in and spoke to me. I was giving scholarships to nearly every client and also kicking paying clients out when it was obvious that they weren't taking the program seriously. If the business was going to survive, I was going to need to keep more insured clients in treatment even if they weren't following the rules. I listened and made the changes that Ryan and Brown had recommended. I was passionate about what we were doing. We proved that when your heart is in something, it turns to gold. We paid the loan back to Brown in six months.

Things were going incredibly well. I loved going to work. I loved my coworkers, who were caring and fun to be around. We laughed all the time. Together we all grew into the business, and the business grew with us as we became masters of our jobs and working together as a team. We had success after success, helping people one at a time to stay in recovery from drug addiction, heal their pasts, and reenter the world. Of course, we also had a few losses that hit hard, but overall we were making a difference.

I was still talking to my dad when Ryan and I were in the process of getting Journey to Joy off the ground. I took my dad on a tour of the building in Fort Lauderdale and told him what we were going to do, what offices would go where, the places that we were creating for clients, and the overall program we were planning. I turned around, and he was crying. He said, "I'm just so proud of you." It was a rare moment when my dad was genuine and kind, when he actually saw me and cared about my life.

Then the treatment world changed: Treatment facilities went corporate. We were in competition with large, institutionally run centers. In 2015 we merged with Apollo Behavioral Health Organization, which had four facilities. We kept our name, Journey to Joy, and worked under the Apollo umbrella, which is still in business today. Chris and I had just had twin girls, Ava and Sadie, and I moved from a job working intensely with clients to sitting on the board of the new company, giving me time to be a mother. In 2017, five years after we'd first started Journey to Joy, we sold Apollo Behavioral Health Organization to a large corporation. We were one of the last holdouts. The whole industry was changing.

When I got my share of the money from the sale of the business, I said to myself, "I think I made it." All that hard work, those eighty-hour work weeks, the counseling, meetings, administrating, answering calls at three o'clock in the morning to hear the voice of a teenager who had relapsed asking if I could pick her up outside a Dunkin Donuts had all paid off. Ava and Sadie were now two years old and the light of my life, and Chris and I could retire—at least temporarily—and concentrate fully on being a family.

Not everyone fared well. Brown relapsed while we were in the process of selling Apollo Behavioral Health Organization. He made promises that he never intended to keep to employees who had dedicated themselves to their work for years. They left the table with nothing. Alex Brown left with millions of dollars.

* * *

My sponsor's sponsor used to say that the most amazing thing about people in recovery is that we're such different people but we all share the same feelings. I have come to understand that all of these negative feelings and the subsequent behaviors—anger, jealousy, resentment, lying—are faces of one emotion: fear. Fear manifests differently for different people. It causes some people to ignore situations, as Sharon did—she was afraid what she would find out if she confronted me; it stirs other people into rage.

Maybe this is not only true of people in recovery, but of all people who have been through traumatic experiences, or maybe all people in general—our negative emotions and behaviors are based in fear. In writing this book, I came to see that Sharon and I have many of the same emotions: fear and related anger. But we act on those feelings in very different ways. Although everyone comes to recovery with the same emotions, in order to heal, you must understand where your personal emotions are coming from, see how you are processing and dealing with them, and make a choice to be a better person.

Recovery is an ongoing process. In early recovery I made a lot of mistakes, but I was also fortunate to meet a lot of good people who encouraged and taught me. I learned from watching others and from looking honestly at my own behavior and feelings. I gradually grew into the person who I wanted to be. The empathy that had been with me since childhood, that had at times been a burden, became one of my greatest strengths. I learned to connect, and reconnect, with people in healthy ways.

CHAPTER FOURTEEN

A Room for Fish

Sharon

Healing doesn't mean the damage never existed. It means the damage no longer controls your life.
—Akshay Dubey

When Lisa first entered treatment, I was still angry with her. It was in part the accumulation of so many years of watching and being a victim of her destructive behavior. Those years had worn away at me. I not only felt annoyed by her behavior, betrayed by her constant lying, and fearful that she was so out of control, but I also hated myself for being the kind of person who was impatient and suspicious. I got to a point where I not only hated Lisa's behavior but very nearly disliked her. It was a sickening feeling. I felt that I didn't know my own sister.

I was also angry because after the intervention Lisa didn't go directly into rehab but went to live with Mom and continued a stream of irresponsible and self-centered behavior. When she finally entered detox in New Jersey, I checked out. At that point in my life, I was an expert at compartmentalizing and tuning things out. I told myself that I was no longer needed: Mom and I had gotten Lisa to a good place; now Lisa was in a detox center, and the center would assure that she got better.

As terrible as it is to say, when Lisa left New Jersey to go into treatment in Florida, I was glad that she was gone—not only sequestered to a medical facility but in an entirely different state. The physical distance between us dictated that she was no longer my responsibility. I allowed myself to stop worrying. I wanted her to get better, but what I wanted even more was for the whole nightmare to not have happened, for it to have been a dream. I tried to erase Lisa's addiction with silence. I didn't speak about it or Lisa's subsequent treatment to my friends or coworkers. I just couldn't believe that my reality involved my sister going to rehab. I didn't want to acknowledge her addiction out loud and let it take physical form in my voice.

I got two phone calls from Lisa while she was in Florida that marked two of the hardest days of my life—along with the day that Mom and I held our intervention for Lisa. Lisa was kicked out of rehab. It ended up being a momentary setback, but when it happened, it was devastating. She was basically on the streets with nothing. I had been warned by therapists and specialists not to enable her. She called crying and begging me for help. "No," I had to say. I paid for her cab fare to a shelter with my credit card but refused to give her a penny more. I had to totally turn my back on her. It was terrible.

The other phone call came months later, after Lisa had returned to treatment. She was in a bad place and thought that she might relapse. She didn't yet have a sponsor. I was her lifeline, her stand-in therapist, makeshift sponsor. I talked her through her panic. "It's going to be okay," I said again and again. "You're going to be okay."

We stayed on the phone for a long time, talking about how she was feeling, and then talking about nothing: Florida versus New Jersey weather, the fate of people we'd known in high school, the unlikely plot of a book I was reading. We kept talking until we were both sure that she wasn't going to use. I was exhausted when we finally hung up and exhausted for days after. I dealt with these things in the silent void that I had created, not reaching out to friends for support and hiding the truth of Aunt Lisa's whereabouts and condition from my children and Anthony's extended family.

* * *

While Lisa was in recovery and then starting her life anew in Florida, my life went on in New Jersey. After taking a couple years off following James's birth, I went back to work part-time for a couple of years, then returned to full-time teaching in a fifth-grade class in Glen Rock when James was in kindergarten, Daniella was in first grade, and Joe was in third. Many of the people who Lisa and I grew up with still live in Glen Rock, and now I teach their children and meet with them at student-teacher conferences or school meetings. It's a lesson about small communities and communal ways of forgiving but never forgetting. If I could have told all these people when we were young that when we were adults, I would be their child's fifth-grade teacher, none of us would have believed it. Our roles have dramatically changed, but the setting of the elementary school makes the memories of our own childhoods seem close. It is a reason to be kind to everyone all the time—you never know whom you will bump into again later, or what role they could play in your life.

Teaching has changed a great deal over the course of my career to accommodate testing and standardization, but the elementary school in Glen Rock where I work still feels like a family. I love my job and my coworkers.

Probably because I am a teacher, education is a major focus for all three of my children. Of course, they have all grown up to be their own people, but I sometimes see in them things that remind me of Anthony, Lisa, my mom, me, and even some of the good things about my dad.

As of this writing, my oldest son is a freshman in college. It has been amazing to be a mother and to raise children who have grown up to be wonderful people who are so different from one another and also different from Anthony and me. In writing this book with my sister, I have thought about my own children as siblings, like Lisa and me, who have grown up so differently than us, negotiating their emotions and challenges in their own ways.

It has also been amazing to have Lisa back in my life as the sister whom I can confide in and want to spend time with rather than avoid and disregard. My relationship with Lisa has gone from one of a sort of emotional estrangement where I distrusted everything that she said and was embarrassed to be related to and associated with her to now, when I actually seek her advice about large and small matters in my life. Lisa and I talk nearly every day. We are very close. If I need to talk to somebody, or need to bounce an idea around, there is nobody in the world whom I would go to besides Lisa.

It took me a long time to get here. For years, even after Lisa was in treatment, I did not completely trust her. I scrutinized the things she told me, looking for the flaws that would reveal the greater falsehood. Gradually I saw that she had truly changed. Now she is a nearly impossibly positive person, and her positivity is genuine. I enjoy being around her. She can be counted on. She can be trusted.

After treatment, as part of Lisa's recovery, she made amends to people to whom she'd done harm while an active addict. She made amends to me, to Mom, and to friends and acquaintances. I think that one of the most difficult apologies that she made was to Anthony. Anthony and I had dealt with Lisa's active addiction differently. I had blinded myself to much of what she had done and made excuses. Anthony had been aware throughout of all the destruction she was causing and had also been helpless to respond so long as I refused to acknowledge the problem. There were times when our disagreements over Lisa very nearly ended our marriage. While my anger with Lisa stemmed from a place of hurt, his was true resentment.

Although it took me a while to let Lisa back into my life completely, I was eager to do so. I wanted my sister back; I knew all the things that Lisa had dealt with as a child and felt empathy for her. Anthony was more reluctant to forgive. He didn't think that Lisa truly understood the damage that she had caused and didn't fully understand the idea of addiction. He stayed angry at Lisa long after I had forgiven her.

When Lisa made amends to Mom and me, we both said something to the tone of "Don't worry about the past. Just keep doing the right thing now." But Anthony let Lisa know that he was angry, and he let her know why. He told her about all of the damage that she had caused—some of which she was aware and some not—and held her accountable fully. He didn't tell her, "It's okay." It was heartbreaking for her but also eye-opening. Even at that point in her life, people were making excuses for her and finding reasons why she wasn't responsible for her own behavior. It was still the easier thing to do—to let Lisa off the hook, to let ourselves off the hook, and to minimize what had happened.

Since that time Lisa has proven herself even to Anthony, who has since forgiven her and accepted her fully into our lives. In small ways, Lisa's role and mine have reversed. It used to be that I was always taking care of Lisa, aware of her blood sugar levels, listening to her upset ramblings, trying to support her as her life fell apart. Now, it is often me calling her in crisis—small crises in comparison to those she used to have. She grounds me when I am upset about something. I don't know what I would do without her in my life.

Last year was a particularly hard time for me. A difficult situation arose in my class, and I knew I would soon be losing my oldest son to college. I would talk to Lisa on my way to work. Her life has changed so much since she sold her business. She was retired—very early—and I was exhausted by teaching. She would tell me about the really busy day she'd had playing tennis and getting her nails done. It was infuriating, but it also brought me so much joy to think that she was finally healthy and doing so well. I would never trade places with Lisa and go through what she went through, even if it garnered me the life she has now. I don't want to be an addict. Lisa battles every single day. She earned and earns everything that she has. She walked a difficult road, then worked hard to build a new life.

Lisa battles every single day. She earned and earns everything that she has. She walked a difficult road, then worked hard to build a new life.

Anthony and I didn't tell our kids about Lisa's addiction until a few years ago, after Lisa sold her business. The Aunt Lisa they knew was in recovery and wonderful, and we wanted them to get to know that Lisa before we told them about that other version of my sister who was an active drug addict. We were also worried that our kids might look at how well Lisa had turned out and think that using drugs, or even being an addict, wasn't really that bad.

Lisa's addiction terrified me to the point that I was strict and absolute with my children when it came to drugs. I never sugar-coated anything. I told them, "If you do drugs, you're going to die." I believed it, in a way. Then I would add, "If the drugs don't kill you, and I find out you're doing drugs, I'll kill you."

So for a while, Lisa's addiction was something we kept in the dark. We didn't lie about it but also didn't actively bring it up. Lately, Lisa has been talking about it more. And now my children also know that Lisa is an addict, although I don't think they understand how bad things really got.

* * *

My family still lives in the same house in Ramsey where we added a family room fourteen years ago, when my kids were small. While writing this book, the space is evolving again, this time to accommodate fish. My youngest son has become a fish enthusiast and wanted to upgrade from the thirty-gallon saltwater tank he has in his room to a ninety-gallon tank that would only fit in the family room.

Now, I am sitting on the sofa in the family room, built before James could walk, staring at the mystical landscape of my son's universe-sized fish tank and the fish that glow with neon stripes and patterns. Above the tank's soft hum is the sound of my daughter peeling tissue paper from the packed Christmas decorations she enthusiastically insists on putting out months before the holiday. I watch her arrange them carefully on the mantle of the fireplace that she just painted to complement the move in furniture required by the addition of the fish tank. My oldest son will be home on his school break soon. Then Lisa and her family will come to town to visit. For a long time, I never imagined that we would get here. This is the family that we were meant to be: this happy, secure, confident, loving family who can't wait to be together. It is because we very nearly did not have this that I am so able to appreciate what we are.

CHAPTER FIFTEEN

Stepmother

Lisa

I am thankful for all of those who said no to me. It's because of them I did it myself.
—Albert Einstein

Six years after I got sober—after I started a successful business, entered a good and lasting relationship, and truly found myself—I had a mental breakdown. It happened when I met my stepchildren. This little boy and girl came into my life, and my entire childhood came flooding back to me.

Chris and I were married seven months after Ryan and I had started Journey to Joy. The marriage made me a stepmother. The word itself has so many negative connotations: *stepmother*. Disney movies have taught us that every stepmother is an evil stepmother.

It is the most difficult role in a family. For whatever reason, families embrace stepfathers, and this was the case with my own stepfather—Bruce was amazing. I don't know why the relationships between stepmothers and stepchildren are often so fraught—my relationship with my stepmother was definitely fraught, as was my dad's relationship with his stepmother—but it seems related to that fierce kind of love that we expect from mothers and perhaps the loyalty that we also expect from both mothers and children toward one another.

I was in therapy for years before Chris and I were married. I had spoken about my childhood and specifically about the way that Janet and my dad had made me feel when I was at their house. I felt like I had worked through those deep feelings of being neglected, unwanted, and unloved by those adults in my life that I depended on. I had come to understand that Janet was jealous and insecure, and that my dad had no idea how to show me love. They didn't know they were doing anything wrong and had no idea that things were so rough for me. Together they normalized their feelings toward me and Sharon, and the way they acted on those feelings. In the short-term it meant that I felt like I didn't matter and wasn't part of their real family; in the long term it led to the sense of abandonment I have felt my whole life.

When I was a child, all that I could do was react to the ways Janet and my dad treated me and made me feel. They had the power and controlled the situation. As an adult I took control of what I could: I accepted what their actions had meant for me and chose my own path forward. I never imagined that I would find myself comparing my own feelings to theirs—especially Janet's—or that I would worry that I was at risk for repeating their behavior. Although I had worked through a lot of my trauma, I had not resolved it entirely. In marrying Chris and becoming a stepmother myself, life was throwing me another challenge and forcing me to examine those dark places in my past that still hid in the shadows of my emotions.

It's difficult even to put into words how I felt when I became engaged to Chris and began to play the role of stepmother. Tommy and Ann came to our house every other weekend, arriving on Friday night and leaving Sunday morning—the same schedule by which Sharon and I had visited our dad and Janet as children. I obsessed over Tommy and Ann's visits, my anxiety growing as their visits approached. I didn't like to be around my them. I started to not like them. When they left, a guilty relief would come over me as I heard myself say in my head, *I don't have to see them again for two weeks.*

It was heart-wrenching to feel that way. I knew that my feelings had nothing to do with Tommy and Ann. They were delightful children. I love them so much now, and I wanted to love them then, but that apprehension was my truth.

I did everything that I could to hide the way that I was feeling, to make Tommy and Ann feel welcome, and to keep from hurting them. Before one visit I went around the house and put up extra pictures of them, adding to the ones that Chris and I already kept, so that they would know that we were not trying to forget or dismiss them. When they went away on a vacation and we did not see them for a month, I decorated their room with balloons to welcome them home. I cheered and cheered every time they walked through the door, "Yay! Tommy and Ann are here!" They seemed to appreciate my efforts. "Thank you so much," Tommy said.

I hoped that they couldn't sense the underlying unease beneath my gestures. I wanted them to feel welcome and wanted, but dealing with my emotions and trying to hide them were exhausting. It was not the same lying that I had done as an active addict, but it drained and diminished me in the same ways.

* * *

Ann's situation especially reminded me of my own childhood. Before Chris and I started dating, but were good friends, Ann had a medical emergency. She was five—one year younger than I had been when admitted to the hospital and diagnosed with juvenile diabetes. Ann suffered from a condition called gastric volvulus, in which the stomach flips out of position. It is a rare condition in humans and almost unheard of in children. Heather was then, and still is, an active addict, which further complicated the situation.

Chris and Heather had been on and off drugs together throughout their relationship. When Heather got pregnant with Tommy, they got married. They were both in their early twenties—still kids. When Ann was born, Heather and Chris entered two different treatment centers. Coincidentally, I met Heather soon after, in treatment when she was sober. She stayed sober for a year but then went through cycles of detox, sometimes treatment, then relapse—a routine that she continues today. Chris and Heather separated when Chris got sober.

For years, I continued to see Heather when she came in and out of detox and treatment centers where I worked. Before I met Chris, I heard Heather talk about him—her terrible ex-husband. She spoke about him as though he were a monster responsible for all of her problems. After Chris and Heather separated, Heather's parents became Tommy and Ann's primary caretakers.

While Ann was going through her struggle with gastric volvulus at five years old, Chris would come to work heartbroken and talk to me about spending days in the hospital with his daughter. Heather was also often there, high and nodding off in a chair in the waiting room. Chris knew that it would be better for his children if Heather were healthy. He offered to help her enter treatment again. "Let's get help," he said. He wanted her to get better.

When she refused, he said for the first time, "If you don't get help, I'm taking you to court."

* * *

Because my childhood mirrored Ann and Tommy's—we are the children of divorce and active addicts—my past returned to me when they entered my life—that painful time in my life that I did not want to remember. I have this strange childhood memory of watching my dad walk down the stairs. He was holding a belt. As he came toward me, I started hysterically crying. My emotion was triggered by, but unrelated to, the situation. My dad was not angry with me; he was not wielding the belt in a threatening way; he had never struck me or been violent with me in any way, and yet in that moment I was certain that he was going to hit me. I was terrified.

"Why are you crying?" he asked me as he put his belt on casually.

I still don't know why I was so afraid. It was an idea or feeling of being afraid, threatened, small, and helpless that I had long held.

That memory came back to me during one of Tommy and Ann's visits when Ann accidentally broke a glass and started crying uncontrollably.

Although neither Chris nor I yelled at her or expressed any anger, and although we had never gotten angry with her for such an accident, she responded as though she expected that we would yell at her, or as though we already had.

"Ann, it's okay, hon," I said.

"Ann, don't worry about it," Chris comforted.

But as I had been responding to some hidden fear that had lain dormant under my surface until invoked by the sight of my dad's belt, Ann was reacting according to her own secret dread.

When I told Sharon about my memory of our dad's belt and how confounded I was by my own reaction, she said, "You were always on your toes. You always wanted to be perfect. You were always worried that you would do something wrong."

It makes sense. It seemed like at my dad's house I could never do anything right. I was never given approval or encouragement by my dad or Janet. I was scrutinized frequently for things I didn't understand or mean. I was on edge. I was waiting to be scolded, to be told that I was no good or had not done good; I was waiting to be punished.

> I always felt the pressure to act happy and to make those around me happy, even while I was dying inside. I was always trying to be who I thought people wanted me to be, and because of that, I never knew who I really was until I went through recovery.

As a child I took on the emotions of others. I always felt the pressure to act happy and to make those around me happy, even while I was dying inside. I was always trying to be who I thought people wanted me to be, and because of that, I never knew who I really was until I went through recovery. I was so concerned with assessing what other people wanted and working to meet their expectations that I didn't consider what I wanted. I didn't know anything about myself. A teacher would ask me what my favorite song was, and I wouldn't know.

Having Tommy and Ann around meant that I was constantly reliving moments from my past: the memory of feeling terrified when I saw my dad walking down the stairs with the belt, shrinking under a look from Janet, or staring at a meal that I didn't want to eat but couldn't reject without risking conflict. Their presence cracked me open and forced me to look at my past. I had no idea how angry I still was.

* * *

When Chris and I were engaged, we came to a pivotal moment involving our time with his kids. He and Heather went to court to resolve custody issues. In addition to being an active drug addict, Heather is also a pathological liar—Chris suspects that she has a borderline personality disorder. In the same way that she had lied to me about Chris to get my sympathies, she has lied about large and small things to get attention, assistance, benefits, and recusal. I have several times heard Chris's family talk about her; it is the way I imagine my family talked about me when I was in active addiction.

During the custody hearing, Heather lied in court in order to keep Chris from getting custody of his children or visitation rights. It was unimaginable. She made false accusations that claimed that Chris was abusive and predatory. We had not come to court prepared for her malicious slander and was not equipped to defend himself beyond denying what Heather said. The justice system generally treated Chris unfairly during the custody battle, and the judge that day was awful to Chris. He brought up Chris's past as a drug user and disregarded his recovery.

When we got home from court, Chris fell to his knees and cried. "I love my kids, but I can never see them again," he said. "I can't go through that again. I don't want to feel like this."

It was my out. Chris was relenting. He had accepted that he would not have a relationship with these two children whose presence had caused me to break down emotionally. All that I had to do was tell him that it was okay to give up, that he had done what he could, and we could move on.

But when Chris said that he would never see his kids again, it seemed wrong. Something came over me.

Without pause or thought, I said what I wished my dad had said about me. "Chris, we're going to fight for these kids. They're going to know how much you love them." I heard myself speak the words and almost couldn't even believe they were my own. "We're going to fight," I said. "And we're going to show the court system that Heather is a liar and a mess."

And we did. We got a great lawyer and—after a year of fighting—we won. Chris did not get full custody but because Heather was and is still in active addiction, the children continue to live with their grandparents, and Chris was given regular visitation. At that point Chris and I were married. Tommy was eleven and Ann was nine.

People say you must do whatever it takes to see your kids. Chris truly did that. He fought for his right to stay in Tommy and Ann's lives. Chris didn't have the tens of thousands of dollars that it would have cost to present the judge with all of the evidence that had been accumulating against Heather and her case for custody over the previous eight years—including the fact that the children had been living with her parents, not her—but he presented what he was able. Her actions, behaviors, and lies were unfathomable. You can't really understand a situation like this unless you've been through it yourself. Chris fought for his kids, and eventually he had to be done fighting and start just being their father. He prays that one day his children will understand what happened and not blame him for the difficult things that happened in their childhoods. Heather and Chris's relationship was tumultuous, just as my mom and dad's was, but I believe there are no real mistakes in life. Beautiful things come from mistakes. For my mother, it was Sharon and me, and for Chris, it was Tommy and Ann.

* * *

That day when I told Chris not to give up fighting for his children, I acted the way that I wished I felt: as though I had a desire to do everything I could to keep Tommy and Ann in our family. It was genuine but not an honest reflection of my feelings. Tommy and Ann continued to bring forth emotions that took hold of me in devastating ways. I realized how unfair it was to associate the terrible feelings from my childhood with my stepchildren. As a child I'd had no control over my situation and my responses were limited; as an adult I needed to take control and shape my reality.

I didn't want to be anything like my models of a stepmother: my own stepmother and my dad's. I didn't want to be cold or rude or uncaring or dismissive. I was terrified of what I was feeling and of what I might become. I refused to be that kind of person. I had to stop the cycle.

I started looking for help. I got a book about being a stepmother, hoping that it could give me insight into dealing with my emotions. It said: If you don't like your stepchildren, you need to put this book down and go get therapy. I started seeing a therapist.

"I think I'm having a nervous breakdown," I said to my therapist. I was thirty-eight years old, sober, and falling apart all over again.

My therapist said, "Don't worry. You're early. Nervous breakdowns usually happen when people are forty-five."

Talking about my stepchildren, my new role as a stepmother, and my own childhood helped me to sort out and understand my feelings, but it was really watching Chris with his kids that made me realize the obvious: Those kids were not me. When I first met Tommy and Ann, I could only see them as reflections of the sad child that I had been. When I looked at their smiles, I hoped they were genuine, but feared they are the same desperate attempts that I had presented at their ages. The truth, of course, is that they were and are their own people. Chris is nothing like my dad. He is incredibly good to his kids. He hugs them, he tells them he loves them, and he makes time and space for them in his life. I saw him with his children, and I realized that, although there were things that I had in common with Tommy and Ann, their situation was different than mine. I am not them, and they are not who I was. They will go on to have their own lives. They have their own stories and their own demons.

When I truly knew that my stepchildren were not me, I saw that my role in their lives could be one of an understanding caretaker offering love and help. They have a struggle ahead of them. Their mother has been in active addiction their whole lives. They've never lived with either parent. They're constantly hiding and lying. They are going through their own drama, and they need support. It was hard at first, but now, along with Chris, I work diligently to be a constant force of nurturing and love for Tommy and Ann.

* * *

In 2015 Chris and I had twin girls, Ava and Sadie. Our lives completely changed for the better. I got to experience motherhood, and Chris got another chance at fatherhood. He was with me when the girls were born. He wasn't on drugs. He saw the whole thing. He is so appreciative of being involved in our daughters' lives because he knows that he got a second chance.

Ava and Sadie are the best thing that ever happened to me. I can't begin to explain the many profound ways that they have transformed and improved my life and my person. Being a mother is the most rewarding and exhausting position I've ever had in my life. The love that I feel for my daughters is both satisfying and overwhelming. They are my joy.

There is still room in our lives—mine, Chris's, and now Ava and Sadie's—for Tommy and Ann, although now that they are teenagers, they have their own social lives and have less time to spend with us. Their situation continues to be complicated as they work to navigate—and often become complicit in—their mother's lies and drama.

Chris and I hope that one day Tommy and Ann will understand the situation. For now we take peace in knowing that their grandparents are providing a safe and loving home, something for which we will be eternally grateful. We love Tommy and Ann and do what we can to keep them close.

It is difficult to explain the bliss of being in recovery. Because I spent so much of my life being deeply sad, I truly feel and appreciate being happy. Because I spent so many years being distant from myself and the world, I value being passionate and engaged so fully. Because I was so often afraid, I delight in the sense of peace and calm that resides in me now. When I am sad and angry, I can actually let myself realize those emotions and process them.

Because I spent so many years being distant from myself and the world, I value being passionate and engaged so fully. Because I was so often afraid, I delight in the sense of peace and calm that resides in me now.

I am a whole person.

I know how fortunate I was to get a second chance. Every moment of every day, I embrace that opportunity. I live my life. I love my children. I love my stepchildren. I love my husband and all of my family and friends. I am present and awake and bright.

CONCLUSION

So much is clear in hindsight. In the moment, when you are in active addiction or when you are dealing with someone who is in active addiction, you are in survival mode. You are enduring one moment and then the next. You are reacting rather than taking control.

To Lisa, it seemed true that she was only harming herself and that she had a right to do so. Interference from anyone did not seem like an act of aid but rather of aggression. To Sharon, trying to support Lisa seemed the right thing to do, even as that support became a kind of disconnected maintenance. The truth was that Lisa was hurting people around her in large and small ways and most deeply injuring the people who loved her best. The truth was also that supporting Lisa was often an avoidance of confrontation and enabling bad behavior and choices rather than forcing Lisa to honestly assess and deal with her problem.

It was really when Lisa made amends that she had to acknowledge and be accountable for her past behavior. To be accountable is to be responsible for and able to justify your own actions. We can see now that neither of us was truly healed until we were able to acknowledge and be accountable for the mistakes that we made. This isn't to say that if we had a second chance, we would do anything differently or be able to do anything differently. There are some things that you can only fully understand in hindsight, and while our journey has been difficult, its rewards have been invaluable.

To make amends is to balance your past wrongdoings with actions and behaviors in the present that offer compensation. Perhaps this is not a bad way to live a life, aware always of ways that you can be a positive force in the world, accepting that you are fallible and working to be the best person you can be.

Early in recovery, Lisa said to our stepfather, Bruce, that she couldn't help her behavior because "This is what alcoholics and addicts do."

Bruce sat her down and said, "You don't think I'm afraid? You don't think that I get scared that the decisions that I make in life may be wrong? It's called being a human being. All human beings are unsure and afraid of the decisions they make."

In writing this book, we sisters have come to see how much people have in common. We manifest our emotions in different and personal ways, but at their root, these are still the same emotions. While we took diverging paths and were directed by opposing responses to similar situations, we largely always wanted the same things. And the things that we want, and fear, and regret, are mainly shared human desires, and fears, and feelings.

No one is alone.

Addiction is a difficult disease to understand and live with. Childhood trauma is equally amorphous and shattering. Both can be survived and can lead to reflection that ultimately makes people stronger. The first step to taking control of either is recognizing their existence. The second step is acknowledging them in your life. We hope that our book helps people to see and understand this type of suffering so that they can recognize it in their own lives or the lives of those close to them. We hope that our story shows those suffering that they are not alone and gives them the courage to acknowledge their pain and find their ways to better lives, as we did.

We are finishing this book in the shadow of the COVID-19 pandemic, which has sent people across the world into lockdown and quarantine, stressed our economic and essential structures, and caused fear and anxiety for people on many levels. Sharon is still teaching and working diligently on a daily basis to create an online curriculum for her students that both helps them to process this historic phenomenon and continue learning. Lisa continues to work on boards—via Zoom meetings—and with organizations that care for our society's most vulnerable people and consider how they are coping with this stressful situation. She can't help but see the similarities between COVID-19 and addiction, two illnesses to which anyone—regardless of race, religion, economic status, and age—can fall victim. COVID-19 is a great equalizer that shows is that human beings everywhere are connected and dependent upon one another. Although the pandemic has been and continues to be terrible on so many levels, we believe that good always wins—our lives are proof of this. Something positive will come out of this experience. It will teach us—as families, communities, nations, and a world—and in the end we will be better for having gone through it. This belief has helped us recover and continues now to help us get through each day.

CPSIA information can be obtained
at www.ICGtesting.com
Printed in the USA
JSHW031814101120
9481JS00001B/24